# Toll House
# Heritage Cookbook

*A collection of favorite dessert recipes*

## Revised Edition

A RUTLEDGE BOOK

*I wish to express my thanks to Alexis Cole Shantz, Manager — Public Relations, for her assistance in coordinating this project; and to Ann N. Dries, Director, Home Economics and Consumer Service, and her staff, Janet Andreas, Jo Ann Billowitz, Wendy Kaye and Lynne M. Paino, for developing and testing all the recipes in this book.*

*Former Group Product Manager*
*Baking Products*
*The Nestlé Company, Inc.*

*Appreciation and thanks are also extended to the following people for their assistance in revising the book: Marie-Claude Stockl, Director — Corporate Affairs; Toll House Morsel brand group — Robert P. Wennerholt, Phyllis A. Traver and especially Meredith B. Galassi, for coordinating the revision; and to Adair Sampogna, Manager — Consumer Affairs, and staff members Ann Dries, Wendy Kaye, Jeanne Murphy and Anna Matina, for developing and testing all new recipes in this book.*

*Photography by Gordon E. Smith*

*Cover art and illustrations by Lauren Rosen*

*Many of the photographs in this cookbook were taken at Old Bethpage Village Restoration, a living museum in the county of Nassau, Long Island, New York, that depicts the life and work styles of a rural village in the eighteenth and nineteenth centuries.*

*Published by Rutledge Books, Inc.*
*300 Mercer Street, New York, N.Y. 10003*

Library of Congress Catalog Card Number: 80–12851
ISBN: 0-87469-043-9

*First Printing: August, 1980*
Printed in Italy

Distributed by M.A.G.I.C. Inc., 1950 Craig Rd., St. Louis, Mo. 63146

# Contents

Introduction                                    4
Cooking with Chocolate                          6
Helpful Baking Basics                           7
In the Toll House Tradition                     8
Candies and Confections                        20
Cookies and Snacks                             34
Cakes and Breads                               62
Pies                                           80
Chilled and Frozen Desserts                    92
Special Occasion Desserts                     104
Sauces, Frostings and Glazes                  118
Index                                         127

# Introduction

Our heritage cookbook celebrates over a half century of great American desserts.

It all started in the thirties. In 1930, Ruth Wakefield, proprietress of the Toll House Inn, was experimenting with a favorite Colonial cookie recipe. She cut a bar of Nestlé Semi-Sweet chocolate into tiny bits and, expecting them to melt, added them to the cookie dough. Instead of melting into the dough, the bits of chocolate held their shape, softening just slightly to a creamy texture. The Toll House Cookie was born.

With Mrs. Wakefield's permission, Nestlé put her recipe on the wrapper of their semi-sweet chocolate bar; later, looking for ways to make it easier for bakers to make their "bits," Nestlé produced a special scored chocolate bar accompanied by a chopper for cutting the chocolate into small pieces. In 1939, Nestlé offered little pieces of chocolate in convenient, ready-to-use packages—and the very first semi-sweet real chocolate morsels were introduced to American bakers. In the forties, Mrs. Wakefield sold all legal rights to use of the Toll House trademark to Nestlé. The rest is history. Nestlé has brought the Toll House recipe and products to millions of homes through advertising, promotions and recipe booklets.

Today, Nestlé Toll House Semi-Sweet Chocolate Morsels are still the best-selling chocolate pieces in America and Toll House Cookies are still America's favorite.

Our cookbook is an inspired collection of treats and desserts of all kinds and for every occasion—or for no occasion at all except to satisfy a sweet tooth. Desserts for lunch boxes—and for opulent buffets. Sinfully rich candies. Holiday creations. Cookies kids of all ages dream about. And best of all, most of the recipes are chocolate: Nestlé is synonymous with the world's favorite flavor.

Nestlé Toll House Semi-Sweet Chocolate Morsels and Nestlé Choco-bake Unsweetened Baking Chocolate Flavor packets are the heart of most of these luscious recipes. In addition, there are plenty of dessert and candy recipes made with other popular flavors: Nestlé Butterscotch Flavored Morsels and Nestlé Milk Chocolate Morsels.

Moreover, the two newest Nestlé morsels have inspired even more delicious recipes. The special Toll House Cake recipes, made with Nestlé Little Bits Semi-Sweet Chocolate, bring that great Toll House taste to cakes. And, new Nestlé Peanut Butter Morsels provide a burst of smooth, creamy peanut butter taste in every bite.

In our heritage cookbook you'll find old-fashioned favorites you've often asked for as well as some new temptations. The versatility of chocolate is deliciously demonstrated, for example, by our breakfast breads—plus the many surprising new ways that we've discovered to display this rich and delectable ingredient.

We invite you to celebrate with us in the best possible way: Come into the kitchen and rediscover the timeless joy of baking and dessert-making.

# Cooking with Chocolate

**Chocolate "bloom":** Chocolate has a high content of cocoa butter. When stored at temperatures that fluctuate from hot to cold, chocolate can develop "bloom"—a grey film caused by the cocoa butter rising to the surface. While this dulls the rich brown chocolate color, it does not affect the taste. When the chocolate melts, it regains its attractive color—don't hesitate to use it.

**Storing chocolate:** Keep chocolate in a cool, dry place. Storage temperature should be between 60° and 78°F., with relative humidity at less than 50%. Chocolate can be refrigerated, but wrap it tightly so it won't absorb odors. Airtight wrapping will also help prevent moisture from condensing on the chocolate when removed from the refrigerator. Chocolate becomes hard and very brittle when cold, so allow it to come to room temperature before using.

**About Nestlé Milk Chocolate Morsels:** *Don't* use Nestlé Milk Chocolate Morsels in baked desserts that do not call for *melting* the morsels before blending them in. The milk causes them to become hard when they are baked. You may substitute Nestlé Milk Chocolate Morsels for Nestlé Toll House Semi-Sweet Chocolate Morsels in recipes such as frosting or sauces that call for melting the morsels. Nestlé Milk Chocolate Morsels can be melted in a dry double boiler or a microwave oven according to the instructions below for melting Nestlé Toll House Semi-Sweet Chocolate Morsels.

**About Nestlé Choco-bake Unsweetened Baking Chocolate Flavor:** Convenient liquid Nestlé Choco-bake Unsweetened Baking Chocolate Flavor can be used in any recipe calling for unsweetened chocolate or cocoa powder. It's packaged in handy 1-ounce envelopes. One ·envelope Nestlé Choco-bake equals 1 square unsweetened baking chocolate or ¼ cup cocoa powder.

**About Nestlé Butterscotch Flavored Morsels and Peanut Butter Morsels:** Melt according to the instructions below for melting Nestlé Toll House Semi-Sweet Chocolate Morsels.

## About Melting Chocolate

**Important:** The smallest drop of moisture can cause melted chocolate to become lumpy—even a wet spoon, or steam from the double boiler. If this should occur, stir in 1 tablespoon vegetable shortening for every 3 ounces chocolate. Do not use butter as it contains water.

**Yield:** One 12-ounce package (2 cups) Nestlé Toll House Semi-Sweet Morsels equals 1 cup melted chocolate.

**Top of Stove Method:** Place Nestlé Toll House Semi-Sweet Morsels in the top of a dry, clean double boiler. Place over hot — not boiling — water. Stir occasionally until smooth.

**Microwave Oven Method:** *To melt one 6-ounce package (1 cup) Nestlé Toll House Semi-Sweet Chocolate Morsels:* Place morsels in a dry 2-cup glass measuring cup. Microwave on high 1 minute; stir. Microwave on high 1 minute longer. Stir until chocolate is smooth.

*To melt one 12-ounce package (2 cups) Nestlé Toll House Semi-Sweet Chocolate Morsels:* Place morsels in a dry 4-cup glass measuring cup. Microwave on high 2 minutes; stir. Microwave on high 1 minute longer. Stir until chocolate is smooth.

# Chocolate Conversion Chart

| When recipe calls for: | You may use: |
| --- | --- |
| 1 oz. (1 square) unsweetened baking chocolate | 1 envelope (1 oz.) Nestlé Choco-bake Unsweetened Baking Chocolate Flavor. *Or* 3 oz. (½ cup) Nestlé Toll House Semi-Sweet Chocolate Morsels; *decrease* shortening (1 T.) and sugar (¼ cup) |
| 3 oz. (3 squares) semi-sweet baking chocolate | 3 oz. (½ cup) Nestlé Toll House Semi-Sweet Chocolate Morsels |
| ¼ cup unsweetened cocoa powder | 1 envelope (1 oz.) Nestlé Choco-bake Unsweetened Baking Chocolate Flavor. *Or* 3 oz. (½ cup) Nestlé Toll House Semi-Sweet Chocolate Morsels; *decrease* shortening (1 T.) and sugar (¼ cup) |

# Ingredient Substitutions

| When recipe calls for: | You may substitute: |
| --- | --- |
| 1 t. baking powder | ¼ t. baking soda + ⅝ t. cream of tartar, *or* ¼ t. baking soda + ½ cup buttermilk or sour milk (to replace ½ cup liquid called for in recipe) |
| 1 cup butter | 1 cup margarine *or* 1 cup hydrogenated shortening + ½ t. salt |
| 1 cup buttermilk or sour milk | 1 T. vinegar or lemon juice plus enough sweet milk to equal 1 cup (let stand 5 minutes), *or* 1¾ t. cream of tartar + 1 cup sweet milk |
| 1 cup corn syrup | 1 cup sugar + ¼ cup liquid* |
| 1 cup heavy cream | ⅓ cup butter + about ¾ cup milk |
| 1 cup honey | 1¼ cups sugar + ¼ cup liquid* |
| 1 cup brown sugar | 1 cup white sugar + ¼ cup molasses |
| 1 cup whole milk | ½ cup evaporated milk + ½ cup water, *or* 1 cup reconstituted nonfat dry milk + 2½ t. butter or margarine |

*Use liquid called for in the particular recipe.*

# About All-Purpose Flour

Our recipes call for "all-purpose flour." Almost all flours sold today have been *presifted* and should not be sifted again at home before measuring.

# About Preheated Ovens

All recipes in this cookbook have been developed, tested and timed using ovens that have been preheated for approximately 10 minutes. With some recipes that have brief baking times, such as cookies, the preheating is critical.

# In the Toll House Tradition

*Mrs. Wakefield knew what she was doing when she mixed her first batch of Toll House Cookies. Using a time-tested Colonial recipe, she made her dough from just the right amounts of golden brown sugar, farm-fresh eggs and rich creamery butter. Into the finished batter she stirred her own addition—bits of semi-sweet chocolate chopped from a bar of Nestlé's chocolate. The result was the Nestlé Toll House Cookie, a buttery, brown-sugary delight laced with rich spurts of creamy Nestlé Semi-Sweet Chocolate in every bite.*

*The Nestlé Toll House Cookie went on to become America's favorite cookie. The Toll House Semi-Sweet Chocolate Morsels produced today are made from the same rich chocolate as the bar that Mrs. Wakefield used. And because we know how much people love the taste of this unique combination of ingredients, we've created a variety of dessert recipes based on the taste and texture of the original Nestlé Toll House Cookie. In this chapter you'll find not only a number of delectable variations of the basic cookie, but some special treats and surprises, too.*

# *Original Toll House Cookies*

2¼   cups all-purpose flour
1   measuring teaspoon baking soda
1   measuring teaspoon salt
1   cup butter, softened
¾   cup sugar
¾   cup firmly packed brown sugar
1   measuring teaspoon vanilla extract
2   eggs
1   12-ounce package (2 cups) Nestlé Toll House Semi-Sweet
   Chocolate Morsels
1   cup chopped nuts

Preheat oven to 375°F. In a small bowl, combine flour, baking soda and salt; set aside. In a large bowl, combine butter, sugar, brown sugar and vanilla extract; beat until creamy. Beat in eggs. Gradually add flour mixture; mix well. Stir in Nestlé Toll House Semi-Sweet Chocolate Morsels and nuts. Drop by rounded teaspoonfuls onto ungreased cookie sheets. Bake 8 to 10 minutes.

Makes 100 2-inch cookies

## *VARIATIONS OF ORIGINAL TOLL HOUSE COOKIES*

**PAN COOKIE VARIATION:** *Prepare Toll House Cookie dough as directed. Spread into greased 15x10x1-inch baking pan. Bake at 375°F. for 20 minutes. Cool; cut into thirty-five 2-inch squares.*

Note: *Recipe may be divided in half (use a 6-ounce package of Nestlé Toll House Semi-Sweet Chocolate Morsels; halve the amounts of all other ingredients). Spread dough into greased 9-inch square baking pan. Bake at 375°F. for 20 to 25 minutes. Cool; cut into about sixteen 2-inch squares. For a crisper pan cookie, spread dough into greased 13x9x2-inch baking pan. Bake at 375°F. for 12 to 15 minutes. Cool; cut into twenty-four 2-inch squares.* .

**WHOLE WHEAT TOLL HOUSE COOKIES:** *Substitute un-sifted whole wheat flour for either the total amount of flour (2¼ cups) or substitute unsifted whole wheat flour for half the amount of flour (use 1 cup + 2 measuring tablespoons each whole wheat and all-purpose flour). Note: Cookies made with whole wheat flour are darker than traditional Toll House Cookies.*

*Original Toll House Cookies*

# Refrigerator Toll House Cookies

| | |
|---|---|
| 2¼ | cups all-purpose flour |
| 1 | measuring teaspoon baking soda |
| 1 | measuring teaspoon salt |
| 1 | cup butter, softened |
| ¾ | cup sugar |
| ¾ | cup firmly packed brown sugar |
| 1 | measuring teaspoon vanilla extract |
| 2 | eggs |
| 1 | 12-ounce package (2 cups)Nestlé Toll House Semi-Sweet Chocolate Morsels |
| 1 | cup chopped nuts |

In a small bowl, combine flour, baking soda and salt; set aside. In a large bowl, combine butter, sugar, brown sugar and vanilla extract; beat until creamy. Beat in eggs. Gradually add flour mixture; mix well. Stir in Nestlé Toll House Semi-Sweet Chocolate Morsels and nuts. Divide dough in half; wrap both halves separately in waxed paper. Chill 1 hour, or until firm. On waxed paper, shape each dough half into a 12-inch log. Roll up in waxed paper; refrigerate up to 1 week or freeze up to 8 weeks.

To bake, preheat oven to 375°F. Cut each chilled log into twelve 1-inch slices. Cut each slice into 4 quarters. Place on ungreased cookie sheets. Bake 8 to 10 minutes.

Makes 8 dozen cookies

# Toll House Golden Brownies

| | |
|---|---|
| 2 | cups all-purpose flour |
| 2 | measuring teaspoons baking powder |
| 1 | measuring teaspoon salt |
| ¾ | cup butter, softened |
| ¾ | cup sugar |
| ¾ | cup firmly packed dark brown sugar |
| 1 | measuring teaspoon vanilla extract |
| 3 | eggs |
| 1 | 12-ounce package (2 cups) Nestlé Toll House Semi-Sweet Chocolate Morsels |

Preheat oven to 350°F. In a small bowl, combine flour, baking powder and salt; set aside. In a large bowl, combine butter, sugar, dark brown sugar and vanilla extract; beat until creamy. Add eggs, one at a time, beating well after each addition. Gradually add flour mixture; mix well. Stir in Nestlé Toll House Semi-Sweet Chocolate Morsels. Spread evenly into well-greased 15x10x1-inch baking pan. Bake 30 to 35 minutes. Cool completely. Cut into 2-inch squares.

Makes 35 2-inch squares

## *Double Chocolate Brownies*

| | |
|---|---|
| ³/₄ | cup all-purpose flour |
| ¹/₄ | measuring teaspoon baking soda |
| ¹/₄ | measuring teaspoon salt |
| ¹/₃ | cup butter |
| ³/₄ | cup sugar |
| 2 | measuring tablespoons water |
| 1 | 12-ounce package (2 cups) Nestlé Toll House Semi-Sweet Chocolate Morsels, divided |
| 1 | measuring teaspoon vanilla extract |
| 2 | eggs |
| ¹/₂ | cup chopped nuts |

Preheat oven to 325°F. In a small bowl, combine flour, baking soda and salt; set aside. In a small saucepan, combine butter, sugar and water. Bring *just to a boil*, then remove from heat. Add 6-ounces (1 cup) Nestlé Toll House Semi-Sweet Chocolate Morsels and vanilla extract. Stir until morsels melt and mixture is smooth. Transfer to a large bowl. Add eggs, one at a time, beating well after each addition. Gradually blend in flour mixture. Stir in remaining 1 cup Nestlé Toll House Semi-Sweet Chocolate Morsels and the nuts. Spread into greased 9-inch square baking pan. Bake 30 to 35 minutes. Cool completely. Cut into 2¹/₄-inch squares.

Makes 16 2¹/₄-inch squares

# Toll House Treatwiches

2¼ cups all-purpose flour
1 measuring teaspoon baking soda
1 measuring teaspoon salt
1 cup butter, softened
¾ cup sugar
¾ cup firmly packed brown sugar
1 measuring teaspoon vanilla extract
2 eggs
1 12-ounce package (2 cups) Nestlé Toll House Semi-Sweet Chocolate Morsels
1 cup chopped nuts
1 quart ice cream, softened

Preheat oven to 375°F. In a small bowl, combine flour, baking soda and salt; set aside. In a large bowl, combine butter, sugar, brown sugar and vanilla extract; beat until creamy. Beat in eggs. Gradually add flour mixture; mix well. Stir in Nestlé Toll House Semi-Sweet Chocolate Morsels and nuts. Drop by rounded measuring tablespoonfuls onto ungreased cookie sheets. Press dough into 2-inch circles. Bake 10 to 12 minutes. Cool 1 minute; remove from cookie sheets. Cool completely. Spread 2 to 3 measuring tablespoons ice cream onto bottom of one cookie. Top with another cookie. Repeat with remaining cookies. Wrap each ice cream sandwich in aluminum foil or plastic wrap. Freeze until ready to serve.

Makes 21 3-inch ice cream sandwiches

# Toll House Walnut Pie

2 eggs
½ cup all-purpose flour
½ cup sugar
½ cup firmly packed brown sugar
1 cup butter, melted and cooled to room temperature
1 6-ounce package (1 cup) Nestlé Toll House Semi-Sweet Chocolate Morsels
1 cup chopped walnuts
1 9-inch unbaked pie shell
Whipped cream or ice cream (optional)

Preheat oven to 325°F. In a large bowl, beat eggs until foamy; beat in flour, sugar and brown sugar until well blended. Blend in melted butter. Stir in Nestlé Toll House Semi-Sweet Chocolate Morsels and walnuts. Pour into pie shell. Bake 1 hour. Serve warm with whipped cream or ice cream, if desired.

Makes one 9-inch pie

*Toll House Walnut Pie*

# Toll House Cupcakes

2¼     cups all-purpose flour
1½     measuring teaspoons baking soda
1     measuring teaspoon salt
1     measuring tablespoon vinegar
    Whole milk
1     cup butter, softened
1     cup firmly packed brown sugar
½     cup sugar
1     measuring tablespoon vanilla extract
3     eggs
1     12-ounce package (2 cups) Nestlé Little Bits
      Semi-Sweet Chocolate
    Confectioners' sugar (optional)

Preheat oven to 375°F. In a small bowl, combine flour, baking soda and salt; set aside. Place vinegar in 1-cup liquid measure; fill with milk to 1-cup line; set aside. In a large bowl, combine butter, brown sugar, sugar and vanilla extract; beat at medium speed until light and fluffy (about 3 to 5 minutes). Add eggs, one at a time, beating well after each addition. Turn mixer to low. Gradually add flour mixture, one third at a time, alternately with milk. Remove bowl from mixer. Gently fold in Nestlé Little Bits Semi-Sweet Chocolate with a rubber spatula. Spoon into 30 greased or paper-lined muffin pans, filling each about two-thirds full. Bake 15 to 20 minutes. Cool completely. Sprinkle with confectioners' sugar, if desired.

Makes 30 cupcakes

# Golden Peanut Butter Brownies

1     12-ounce package (2 cups) Nestlé Peanut Butter
      Morsels, divided
2¼     cups all-purpose flour
2½     measuring teaspoons baking powder
½     measuring teaspoon salt
1     cup butter, softened
1     cup sugar
1     cup firmly packed brown sugar
1     measuring teaspoon vanilla extract
3     eggs
1     6-ounce package (1 cup) Nestlé Toll House Semi-Sweet
      Chocolate Morsels

Preheat oven to 350°F. Over hot (not boiling) water, melt 1 cup Nestlé Peanut Butter Morsels; stir until smooth. Remove from heat; set aside. In a small bowl, combine flour, baking powder and salt; set aside. In a large bowl, combine butter, sugar, brown sugar and vanilla extract; beat until creamy. Stir in melted peanut butter morsels. Add eggs, one at a time, beating well after each addition. Gradually add flour mixture. Stir in Nestlé Toll House Semi-Sweet Chocolate Morsels. Spread evenly into well-greased 15x10x1-inch baking pan. Bake 30 minutes. Remove from oven; immediately sprinkle top with remaining 1 cup Nestlé Peanut Butter Morsels. Let stand about 5 minutes until morsels become shiny and soft; spread morsels evenly over top of brownies. Cool completely. Cut into 2-inch squares.

Makes 35 2-inch squares

# *Toll House Crumb Cake*

## TOPPING

| | |
|---|---|
| 1 | measuring tablespoon all-purpose flour |
| 1/2 | cup firmly packed brown sugar |
| 2 | measuring tablespoons butter, softened |
| 1/2 | cup chopped nuts |
| 1 | 12-ounce package (2 cups) Nestlé Little Bits Semi-Sweet Chocolate, divided |

## CAKE

| | |
|---|---|
| 2 | cups all-purpose flour |
| 1 | measuring teaspoon baking powder |
| 1 | measuring teaspoon baking soda |
| 1/2 | measuring teaspoon salt |
| 1/2 | cup butter, softened |
| 1 | cup sugar |
| 1 | measuring teaspoon vanilla extract |
| 3 | eggs |
| 1 | cup sour cream |

TOPPING: In a small bowl, combine flour, brown sugar and butter; mix well. Stir in nuts and ½ cup Nestlé Little Bits Semi-Sweet Chocolate; set aside.

CAKE: Preheat oven to 350°F. In a small bowl, combine flour, baking powder, baking soda and salt; set aside. In a large bowl, combine butter, sugar and vanilla extract; mix well. Add eggs, one at a time, beating well after each addition. Gradually add flour mixture alternately with sour cream. Fold in remaining 1½ cups Nestlé Little Bits Semi-Sweet Chocolate. Spread into greased 13x9x2-inch baking pan. Sprinkle topping evenly over batter. Bake 45 to 50 minutes.

Makes 24 2-inch squares

*Toll House Golden Brownies, Toll House Bundt*®*Cake*

# Toll House Bundt® Cake

## NUT TOPPING

- ¼ cup butter, softened
- 2 measuring tablespoons sugar
- ⅔ cup finely chopped nuts

## CAKE

- 2¾ cups all-purpose flour
- 2 measuring teaspoons baking soda
- 1 measuring teaspoon salt
- 1 measuring tablespoon vinegar
  Whole milk
- 1 cup butter, softened
- 1 cup firmly packed brown sugar
- 1 measuring tablespoon vanilla extract
- 4 eggs
- 1 12-ounce package (2 cups) Nestlé Little Bits
     Semi-Sweet Chocolate
  Chocolate Glaze (optional)

TOPPING: In a small bowl, combine butter, sugar and nuts; mix until crumbly. Spoon into well-greased and floured 10-inch fluted tube pan. Chill in refrigerator while preparing cake batter.

CAKE: Preheat oven to 375°F. In a small bowl, combine flour, baking soda and salt; set aside. Place vinegar in a 1-cup liquid measure; fill with milk to 1-cup line; set aside. In a large bowl, combine butter, brown sugar and vanilla extract; beat at medium speed until light and fluffy (about 3 to 5 minutes). Add eggs, one at a time, beating well after each addition. Turn mixer to low. Gradually add flour mixture, one-third at a time, alternately with milk. Remove bowl from mixer. Gently fold in Nestlé Little Bits Semi-Sweet Chocolate with a rubber spatula. Pour batter into prepared pan. Bake for 50 minutes. Check for doneness by inserting toothpick in center of cake. When it comes out clean, cake is done. Cake is a dark golden brown when baked. Loosen edges of cake with spatula; *immediately* invert on cooling rack. Cool cake completely. Drizzle top with Chocolate Glaze (page 42), if desired.

Makes one 10-inch tube or Bundt® cake

# Candies and Confections

Do you remember the delicious Christmas bustle, and how you helped prepare the sweets that welcomed guests and served as loving gifts to family and close friends? The fudge you made on a rainy afternoon that Dad said was the best he ever tasted? And later, the sleep-over where you and your friends trooped into the kitchen to make candy at one in the morning?

These are joyous traditions to continue, pleasures that remain unchanged by the years or fashion. That warmth of yesterday can be captured by the meltingly rich chocolate and butterscotch recipes in this chapter. It is a collection of treats that your whole family will enjoy.

Just one bite of this old-fashioned goodness and the happy memories will come flooding back. And for the youngsters, these new pleasures will become tomorrow's best memories, all to pass on, generation to generation.

# Mocha-Rum Truffles

1    12-ounce package (2 cups) Nestlé Toll House Semi-Sweet
       Chocolate Morsels
1/2  cup butter, softened
4    egg yolks
2    measuring tablespoons rum
2    measuring teaspoons instant coffee
       Confectioners' sugar
       Candied fruit and/or Nestlé Milk Chocolate Morsels and/or
       Nestlé Butterscotch Morsels (all optional)

Melt Nestlé Toll House Semi-Sweet Chocolate Morsels over hot
(not boiling) water; remove from heat but keep chocolate over hot
water. Add butter and egg yolks; beat with wire whisk or fork until
smooth. In a small bowl, combine rum and coffee. Add chocolate
mixture; stir until smooth. Set bowl over an ice bath; chill mixture
20 to 25 minutes, stirring occasionally, until fudgelike in consistency (yet smooth and creamy). Mixture will be quite thick. Fill a
pastry bag fitted with rosette tip with a third of the chocolate mixture. Pipe 1-inch rosettes onto cookie sheets.* Sift confectioners'
sugar over candies. Decorate with candied fruit and/or Nestlé
Milk Chocolate Morsels and/or Nestlé Butterscotch Morsels, if desired. Repeat with remaining chocolate mixture. Let candies
stand at room temperature several hours to season.

Makes 5 dozen 1-inch candies

*Chocolate mixture may be shaped into 1-inch balls, then rolled in
confectioners' sugar.

# Two-Tone Fudge

2 1/2  cups sugar
3/4  cup evaporated milk
1/3  cup butter
1/2  measuring teaspoon salt
3    cups miniature marshmallows
1    6-ounce package (1 cup) Nestlé Butterscotch Flavored
       Morsels
1/2  cup chopped walnuts
1/2  measuring teaspoon maple extract
1    11 1/2-ounce package (2 cups) Nestlé Milk Chocolate Morsels
1    measuring teaspoon vanilla extract

In a large heavy-gauge saucepan, combine sugar, evaporated milk, butter and salt. Cook, stirring constantly, until mixture comes to *full boil*. Boil 7 minutes, stirring constantly. Remove from heat; add marshmallows. Mix until marshmallows melt and mixture is smooth. Place half the hot mixture in a bowl. Add Nestlé Butterscotch Flavored Morsels, walnuts and maple extract. Stir until morsels melt and mixture is smooth; set aside. To remaining mixture, add Nestlé Milk Chocolate Morsels and vanilla extract. Spread chocolate mixture onto foil-lined 9-inch square pan. Pour butterscotch mixture over chocolate layer. Chill in refrigerator until firm (2 to 3 hours). Cut into 1-inch squares.

Makes about 2½ pounds candy

# *Snow Caps*

| | |
|---|---|
| 1 | 12-ounce package (2 cups) Nestlé Toll House Semi-Sweet Chocolate Morsels |
| ¼ | cup dark corn syrup |
| 1 | measuring tablespoon water |
| 1 | cup chopped nuts |
| | Granulated sugar |
| 1 | 8-ounce package cream cheese, softened |
| ⅔ | cup sifted confectioners' sugar |
| 2 | measuring teaspoons vanilla extract |
| | Walnut pieces (optional) |

Over hot (not boiling) water, combine Nestlé Toll House Semi-Sweet Chocolate Morsels, corn syrup and water; heat until morsels melt and mixture is smooth. Stir in chopped nuts. Drop by slightly rounded measuring teaspoonfuls onto waxed paper lined cookie sheets; press flat with bottom of glass dipped in granulated sugar. Chill in refrigerator for 5 minutes. In a small bowl, combine cream cheese, confectioners' sugar and vanilla extract; beat until creamy. Top each chocolate mound with 1 measuring teaspoonful of cream cheese frosting. Garnish with walnut pieces, if desired. Return to refrigerator and chill until firm. Store in airtight container in refrigerator.

Makes 3½ dozen 1½-inch candies

*From top: Two-Tone Fudge*
*Mocha-Rum Truffles, Snow Caps,*
*Chocolate-Mint Fancies*

# *Chocolate-Mint Fancies*

**CHOCOLATE LAYERS**

  **1**   12-ounce package (2 cups) Nestlé Toll House Semi-Sweet Chocolate Morsels, divided

  **4**   measuring tablespoons vegetable shortening, divided

**FONDANT FILLING**

  **5**   measuring tablespoons butter

  **½**   cup light corn syrup

 **4½**   cups sifted confectioners' sugar, divided

  **1**   measuring teaspoon peppermint extract

      Red or green food coloring

CHOCOLATE BOTTOM LAYER: Over hot (not boiling) water, combine 1 cup Nestlé Toll House Semi-Sweet Chocolate Morsels and 2 measuring tablespoons shortening; heat until morsels melt and mixture is smooth. Spread evenly with back of spoon in foil-lined 15x10x1-inch pan. Chill in refrigerator until firm (about 20 minutes). Carefully invert onto waxed paper lined cookie sheet. Gently peel off foil. Return to refrigerator.

FONDANT FILLING: In a large saucepan, combine butter, corn syrup, and half the confectioners' sugar; bring to *full boil*, stiring constantly over *medium-low* heat. Add remaining confectioners' sugar, the peppermint extract and desired amount of food coloring; stir vigorously until well blended (about 3 minutes). Remove from heat. Pour fondant onto greased cookie sheet. Cool long enough to handle (about 5 minutes). Knead until soft (about 2 to 3 minutes). Roll out fondant ⅛ inch thick between two pieces of plastic wrap to form a 15x10-inch rectangle. Remove top sheet of plastic wrap. Carefully invert fondant onto chocolate bottom layer. Remove second sheet of plastic wrap. Chill 15 minutes.

CHOCOLATE TOP LAYER: Over hot (not boiling) water, combine remaining 1 cup Nestlé Toll House Semi-Sweet Chocolate Morsels and 2 measuring tablespoons vegetable shortening; heat until morsels melt and mixture is smooth. Spread evenly over fondant filling. Chill 15 to 20 minutes.

Cut out 24 shapes with a 2-inch cookie cutter. Chill in refrigerator until ready to serve.

Makes 2 dozen 2-inch candies

# Chocolate–Peanut Butter Cups

**CHOCOLATE CUPS**

1   11½-ounce package (2 cups) Nestlé Milk Chocolate Morsels
2   measuring tablespoons vegetable shortening
24  paper gem-size candy liners

**PEANUT BUTTER FILLING**

¾   cup creamy peanut butter
¾   cup sifted confectioners' sugar
1   measuring tablespoon butter, melted

CHOCOLATE CUPS: Over hot (not boiling) water, combine Nestlé Milk Chocolate Morsels and vegetable shortening. Stir until morsels melt and mixture is smooth. Coat inside of 24 candy liners using 1 measuring teaspoon chocolate mixture for each. Keep remaining chocolate warm over very low heat. To coat: Place candy liner in palm of hand; rotate gently, using rubber spatula to push chocolate up sides. Place coated liners in gem pans. Chill in refrigerator until firm (about 30 minutes). Using slightly rounded measuring teaspoonfuls, shape Peanut Butter Filling (below) into balls. Place 1 ball in each cup and press lightly with fingers to flatten. Spoon 1 level measuring teaspoonful melted chocolate mixture on top and smooth over. Return to refrigerator and chill until firm (about 45 minutes) or until hardened. Keep refrigerated until serving.

PEANUT BUTTER FILLING: In a small bowl, combine peanut butter, confectioners' sugar and butter. Mix until well blended.

Makes 24 cups

# Fudge Drops

1    11½-ounce package (2 cups) Nestlé Milk Chocolate Morsels
1¼   cups natural cereal
1    cup salted peanuts
     Whole walnuts, pecans or cashews (optional)

Over hot (not boiling) water, melt Nestlé Milk Chocolate Morsels. Remove from heat; stir in natural cereal and peanuts. Drop by rounded measuring teaspoonfuls onto waxed paper lined cookie sheets. Garnish with whole nuts, if desired. Chill in refrigerator until firm (about 30 minutes).

Makes about 4 dozen candies

# Easy Chocolate Fudge

1  12-ounce package (2 cups) Nestlé Toll House Semi-Sweet
   Chocolate Morsels
1  14-ounce can sweetened condensed milk*
1  cup chopped walnuts
1  measuring teaspoon vanilla extract
   Ready-to-spread frosting (optional)
   Candied cherries (optional)
   Walnut halves (optional)

Over hot (not boiling) water, combine Nestlé Toll House Semi-Sweet Chocolate Morsels and sweetened condensed milk; stir until morsels melt and mixture is smooth. Stir in walnuts and vanilla extract. Spread evenly into foil-lined 8-inch round pan to form a wreath or foil-lined 8-inch square pan. Chill until firm (about 2 hours). Decorate with ready-to-spread frosting, candied cherries and walnut halves, if desired. Cut into 1-inch squares.

Makes 64 1-inch squares

* Not evaporated milk

# Triple Treats

1   11½-ounce package (2 cups) Nestlé Milk Chocolate Morsels
2   measuring tablespoons vegetable shortening
30  vanilla caramels
3   measuring tablespoons butter
2   measuring tablespoons water
1   cup coarsely chopped peanuts

Over hot (not boiling) water, combine Nestlé Milk Chocolate Morsels and vegetable shortening; stir until morsels melt and mixture is smooth. Remove from heat. Pour half of melted chocolate into a foil-lined 8-inch square pan; spread evenly. Refrigerate until firm (about 15 minutes). Return remaining chocolate mixture to *low* heat. Over boiling water, combine caramels, butter and water. Stir until caramels melt and mixture is smooth. Stir in nuts until well blended. Pour into the chocolate-lined pan; spread evenly. Refrigerate until tacky (about 15 minutes). Top with remaining melted chocolate; spread evenly to cover caramel filling. Return to refrigerator and chill until firm (about 1 hour). Cut into 1x2-inch rectangles. Refrigerate until ready to serve.

Makes about 2½ dozen candies

From top: Mix 'Ems, Bourbon Balls,
Marshmallow Cream Fudge

# Bourbon Balls

1   6-ounce package (1 cup) Nestlé Toll House Semi-Sweet
     Chocolate Morsels
3   measuring tablespoons corn syrup
1/2  cup bourbon
2½   cups vanilla wafer crumbs
1/2  cup sifted confectioners' sugar
1   cup finely chopped nuts
     Granulated sugar

Over hot (not boiling) water, melt Nestlé Toll House Semi-Sweet
Chocolate Morsels; remove from heat. Blend in corn syrup and
bourbon. In a large bowl, combine vanilla wafer crumbs, confectioners' sugar and nuts. Add chocolate mixture; mix well. Let
stand about 30 minutes. Form into 1-inch balls. Roll in granulated
sugar. Let season in a covered container for several days.

Makes 4½ dozen 1-inch candies

# Marshmallow Cream Fudge

1   jar marshmallow cream (7½ to 13 ounces)
1½   cups sugar
2/3  cup evaporated milk
1/4  cup butter
1/4  measuring teaspoon salt
1   12-ounce package (2 cups) Nestlé Toll House Semi-Sweet
     Chocolate Morsels
1/2  cup chopped nuts
1   measuring teaspoon vanilla extract

In a medium saucepan, combine marshmallow cream, sugar, evaporated milk, butter and salt, bring to *full boil*, stirring constantly
over moderate heat. *Boil 5 minutes*, stirring constantly over moderate heat. Remove from heat. Add Nestlé Toll House Semi-
Sweet Chocolate Morsels; stir until morsels melt and mixture is
smooth. Stir in nuts and vanilla extract. Pour into foil-lined 8-inch
square pan. Chill in refrigerator until firm (about 2 hours).

Makes 2¼ pounds candy

# Chocolate-Almond Bark

1   11½-ounce package (2 cups) Nestlé Milk Chocolate
     Morsels
1   measuring tablespoon vegetable shortening
½   cup whole almonds
½   cup raisins

Line a 13x9x2-inch baking pan with a sheet of waxed paper about
16 inches long (so that candy can be easily lifted out of the pan).
Over hot (not boiling) water, combine Nestlé Milk Chocolate
Morsels and shortening; heat until morsels melt and mixture is
smooth. Remove from heat and stir in almonds and raisins.
Spread into waxed-paper-lined pan. Chill in refrigerator about 15
minutes; remove and score top with tines of fork to resemble bark.
Return to refrigerator and chill until ready to serve, at least 30 minutes. Before serving, break into bite-size pieces.

Makes 1 pound candy.

# Chocolate Caramel Crowns

1   pound (56) vanilla caramels
2   measuring tablespoons butter
1   measuring tablespoon water
1   11½-ounce package (2 cups) Nestlé Milk
     Chocolate Morsels*
½   cup light corn syrup
2   measuring tablespoons water
     Pecan halves (about 2 cups)

Over boiling water, combine caramels, butter and water; heat until caramels melt and mixture is smooth. Keep warm over boiling
water. Over hot (not boiling) water, combine Nestlé Milk Chocolate Morsels, corn syrup and water; heat until morsels melt and
mixture is smooth. Keep warm over hot water. Place 3 pecan
halves, touching ends in center, on greased cookie sheets. Drop
caramel mixture by ½ measuring teaspoonfuls onto center of
pecans where 3 touch. Drop chocolate mixture over caramel-
nut piece by slightly rounded measuring teaspoonfuls. Chill in
refrigerator until set (about 30 minutes). Refrigerate until ready
to serve.

Makes about 4 dozen candies

* One 12-ounce package (2 cups) Nestlé Toll House Semi-Sweet Chocolate
  Morsels may be substituted for Nestlé Milk Chocolate Morsels.

# Hopscotchers

1    12-ounce package (2 cups) Nestlé Butterscotch Morsels
½    cup light corn syrup
2    measuring tablespoons water
1    measuring tablespoon vegetable shortening
2    3-ounce cans chow mein noodles
4    cups miniature marshmallows or 1 8-ounce package
     chopped dates

Over hot (not boiling) water, combine Nestlé Butterscotch Morsels, corn syrup, water and shortening; heat until morsels melt and mixture is smooth. Transfer to a large bowl. Add noodles; mix well. Cool slightly; fold in marshmallows or dates. Drop by slightly rounded measuring tablespoonfuls onto waxed paper lined cookie sheets. Chill in refrigerator until firm (about 20 minutes).

Makes 4 dozen candies

*PEANUT BUTTER HOPSCOTCHERS: Substitute 1 cup peanut butter for the corn syrup and water.*

# Chocolate-Covered Pretzels

1    6-ounce package (1 cup) Nestlé Toll House Semi-Sweet
     Chocolate Morsels
2    measuring tablespoons corn syrup
2    measuring tablespoons vegetable shortening
1½   measuring teaspoons water
     3-inch twisted pretzels (25 to 30)

Over hot (not boiling) water, combine Nestlé Toll House Semi-Sweet Chocolate Morsels, corn syrup, shortening and water; stir until morsels melt and mixture is smooth. Remove from heat but keep mixture over hot water. Dip pretzels into chocolate mixture to coat evenly. Place pretzels on wire racks set over waxed paper. Chill in refrigerator until coating sets (about 10 minutes). Remove from refrigerator and let stand at room temperature until surface dries (about 1 hour).

Makes 25 to 30 pretzels

*Chocolate-Dipped Fruit*

# Chocolate-Dipped Fruit

1   12-ounce package (2 cups) Nestlé Toll House Semi-Sweet
    Chocolate Morsels*
¼   cup vegetable shortening
    Fresh strawberries, washed and dried, or
    Mandarin orange slices, drained, or
    Pineapple chunks, drained, or
    Maraschino cherries, drained

Over hot (not boiling) water, combine Nestlé Toll House Semi-Sweet Chocolate Morsels and shortening; stir until morsels melt and mixture is smooth. Remove from heat but keep chocolate over hot water.** (If chocolate begins to set, return to heat. Add 1 to 2 measuring teaspoons shortening; stir until smooth.) Dip pieces of desired fruit into chocolate mixture, shaking off excess chocolate. Place on foil-lined cookie sheets. Chill in refrigerator 10 to 15 minutes until chocolate is set. Gently loosen fruit from foil with metal spatula. Chocolate-Dipped Fruit may be kept at room temperature up to 1 hour. If chocolate becomes sticky, return to refrigerator.

Makes 1 cup coating

*One 11½-ounce package (2 cups) Nestlé Milk Chocolate Morsels may be substituted for Nestlé Toll House Semi-Sweet Chocolate Morsels.
**To make in electric fondue pot or skillet, set at low. Combine morsels and shortening. Stir until morsels melt and mixture is smooth. Keep heat set at low. Proceed as directed.

# Creamy Chocolate Fudge

1    jar marshmallow cream (7½ to 13 ounces)
1½   cups sugar
⅔    cup evaporated milk
¼    cup butter
¼    measuring teaspoon salt
1    11½-ounce package (2 cups) Nestlé Milk Chocolate Morsels
1    6-ounce package (1 cup) Nestlé Toll House Semi-Sweet
     Chocolate Morsels
½    cup chopped nuts
1    measuring teaspoon vanilla extract

In a large saucepan, combine marshmallow cream, sugar, evaporated milk, butter and salt; bring to *full boil* over moderate heat, stirring constantly. Boil 5 minutes stirring constantly, over moderate heat. Remove from heat. Add Nestlé Milk Chocolate Morsels and Nestlé Toll House Semi-Sweet chocolate Morsels; stir until morsels melt and mixture is well blended. Stir in nuts and vanilla extract. Pour into foil-lined 8-inch square pan. Chill in refrigerator until firm (about 2 hours).

Makes 2½ pounds candy

# Cookies and Snacks

Just as the smell of sizzling bacon brings back the taste of extra-special breakfasts long ago, so the scent of cookies wafting from the kitchen recalls a score of childhood afternoons. The cry, "Don't slam the door," as you and your friends ran in and out, hands filled with still-warm cookies. The winter days, when hot cocoa, cookies and an apple waited after school or skating. The holidays, when Mom allowed you to stir the dough and shape and decorate it are memories to be cherished for a lifetime.

The cookie jar was always full and the kitchen a center of activity. The hospitable mother always knew where her children were and who was with them. The cookie jar is an open invitation to the youngsters today, just as it was then. Try some of these delicious recipes and find out.

# Triple-Layer Brownies

1   12-ounce package (2 cups) Nestlé Toll House Semi-Sweet
    Chocolate Morsels, divided
1   6-ounce package (1 cup) Nestlé Butterscotch Flavored Morsels
2   cups all-purpose flour
1½  measuring teaspoons baking powder
½   measuring teaspoon salt
1   cup butter, softened
1   cup firmly packed brown sugar
2   measuring teaspoons vanilla extract
3   eggs
1   cup chopped nuts

Preheat oven to 350°F. Melt 1 cup Nestlé Toll House Semi-Sweet
Chocolate Morsels over hot (not boiling) water; set aside. In another pan, melt Nestlé Butterscotch Flavored Morsels over hot (not
boiling) water; set aside. In a small bowl, combine flour, baking
powder and salt; set aside. In a large bowl, combine butter, brown
sugar and vanilla extract; beat until creamy. Add eggs, one at a
time, beating well after each addition. Blend in flour mixture. Stir in
nuts. Divide batter in half; blend melted butterscotch into one half.
Spread into well-greased 13x9x2-inch baking pan. Blend melted
chocolate into remaining batter. Spread evenly over butterscotch
layer. Bake 35 minutes. Remove from oven. Sprinkle remaining 1
cup Nestlé Toll House Semi-Sweet Chocolate Morsels evenly over
top. Let set for about 5 minutes to soften morsels, then spread
evenly over top. Cool completely. Cut in 2x1-inch bars.

Makes 4 dozen 2x1-inch bars

# Butterscotch Brownies

2   cups all-purpose flour
2   measuring teaspoons baking powder
1½  measuring teaspoons salt
1   12-ounce package (2 cups) Nestlé Butterscotch Flavored Morsels
½   cup butter
1   cup firmly packed brown sugar
4   eggs
1   measuring teaspoon vanilla extract
1   cup chopped nuts

Preheat oven to 350°F. In a small bowl, combine flour, baking powder and salt; set aside. Over hot (not boiling) water, combine Nestlé Butterscotch Flavored Morsels and butter; heat until morsels melt and mixture is smooth. Transfer to a large bowl. Stir in brown sugar. Cool 5 minutes. Beat in eggs and vanilla extract. Blend in flour mixture. Stir in nuts. Spread evenly into greased 15x10x1-inch baking pan. Bake 30 minutes. Cool; cut into 2-inch squares.

Makes 35 2-inch squares

# *Cheese Crunchers*

| | |
|---|---|
| 1 | 12-ounce package (2 cups) Nestlé Butterscotch Flavored Morsels |
| 6 | measuring tablespoons butter |
| 2 | cups graham cracker crumbs |
| 2 | cups chopped nuts |
| 2 | 8-ounce packages cream cheese, softened |
| ½ | cup sugar |
| 4 | eggs |
| ¼ | cup all-purpose flour |
| 2 | measuring tablespoons lemon juice |

Preheat oven to 350°F. Over hot (not boiling) water, combine Nestlé Butterscotch Flavored Morsels and butter; heat until morsels melt and mixture is smooth. Transfer to a large bowl; with a fork stir in graham cracker crumbs and nuts until mixture forms small crumbs. Reserve 2 cups crumb mixture for topping. Press remaining mixture into 15x10x1-inch ungreased baking pan. Bake for 12 minutes.

In a large bowl, combine cream cheese and sugar; beat until creamy. Add eggs, one at a time, beating well after each addition. Blend in flour and lemon juice. Pour mixture evenly over hot baked crust. Sprinkle top with reserved crumb mixture. Bake for 25 minutes. Cool completely; cut into 2x1-inch bars. Chill in refrigerator before serving.

Makes 75 2x1-inch bars

*Butterscotch Brownies, Chocolate Snappers,*
*Cream Cheese Ripple Squares*

# Cream Cheese Ripple Squares

**CREAM CHEESE BATTER**

2   3-ounce packages cream cheese, softened
2   eggs
$\frac{1}{4}$   cup sugar
2   measuring tablespoons all-purpose flour
2   measuring tablespoons butter, softened
$\frac{1}{2}$   measuring teaspoon grated orange rind

**CHOCOLATE BATTER**

$\frac{3}{4}$   cup all-purpose flour
$\frac{3}{4}$   cup sugar
$\frac{1}{2}$   measuring teaspoon baking soda
$\frac{1}{2}$   measuring teaspoon salt
$\frac{1}{3}$   cup milk
1   measuring teaspoon vinegar
$\frac{1}{4}$   cup butter, softened
2   envelopes (2 ounces) Nestlé Choco-bake Unsweetened Baking Chocolate Flavor
1   egg
1   measuring teaspoon vanilla extract

CREAM CHEESE BATTER: In a small bowl, combine cream cheese, eggs, sugar, flour, butter and orange rind; beat until creamy. Pour into greased 9-inch square baking pan; set aside. Preheat oven to 350°F.

CHOCOLATE BATTER: In a large bowl, combine flour, sugar, baking soda and salt. Beat in milk, vinegar, butter and Nestlé Choco-bake Unsweetened Baking Chocolate Flavor. Blend in egg and vanilla extract.

Spoon chocolate batter over cream cheese batter. Run knife through to marbleize. Bake 40 to 45 minutes. Cool; cut into 2$\frac{1}{4}$-inch squares.

Makes 16 2$\frac{1}{4}$-inch squares

# Frosted Fudge Brownies

**BROWNIES**

- 1 cup sugar
- 2 eggs
- ½ cup butter, softened
- 2 envelopes (2 ounces) Nestlé Choco-bake Unsweetened Baking Chocolate Flavor
- 1 measuring teaspoon vanilla extract
- ⅔ cup all-purpose flour
- ½ measuring teaspoon baking powder
- ½ measuring teaspoon salt
- ½ cup chopped nuts

**FUDGE FROSTING**

- 1 egg yolk
- 2 measuring tablespoons butter, melted
- 1 envelope (1 ounce) Nestlé Choco-bake Unsweetened Baking Chocolate Flavor
- 1 measuring teaspoon milk
- ½ measuring teaspoon vanilla extract
- 1 cup sifted confectioners' sugar

BROWNIES: Preheat oven to 350°F. In a small bowl combine sugar, eggs, butter, Nestlé Choco-bake Unsweetened Baking Chocolate Flavor and vanilla extract; beat until creamy. Add flour, baking powder and salt; mix well. Add nuts. Spread into greased 8-inch square pan. Bake 30 minutes. Cool completely. Spread with Fudge Frosting (below). Cut into 2-inch squares.

FUDGE FROSTING: In a small bowl, combine egg yolk, butter, Nestlé Choco-bake Unsweetened Baking Chocolate Flavor, milk and vanilla extract; mix until well blended. Gradually add confectioners' sugar; beat until creamy.

Makes 16 2-inch squares

# Banana Pops

- 4 ripe bananas, peeled
- 8 wooden popsicle sticks
- 1 6-ounce package (1 cup) Nestlé Toll House Semi-Sweet Chocolate Morsels or Nestlé Milk Chocolate Morsels
- 1 measuring tablespoon vegetable shortening
  Chopped nuts (optional)
  Shredded coconut (optional)

Cut bananas in halves crosswise. Insert wooden stick in end of each and freeze. Melt Nestlé Toll House Semi-Sweet Chocolate

Morsels and shortening over hot (not boiling) water; stir until smooth. Coat each banana half with chocolate mixture; roll immediately in nuts or coconut, if desired. Wrap each pop in aluminum foil or put in freezer bags and store in freezer.

Makes 8 pops

# *Milk Chocolate Pecan Bars*

## COOKIE BASE
- 1   cup all-purpose flour
- 1/2  cup firmly packed brown sugar
- 1/2  measuring teaspoon baking soda
- 1/4  measuring teaspoon salt
- 1/4  cup butter, softened

## TOPPING
- 1   11½-ounce package (2 cups) Nestlé Milk Chocolate Morsels
- 2   eggs
- 1/4  cup firmly packed brown sugar
- 1   measuring teaspoon vanilla extract
- 1/4  measuring teaspoon salt
- 1   cup chopped pecans, divided

COOKIE BASE: Preheat oven to 350°F. In a large bowl, combine flour, brown sugar, baking soda and salt; mix well. Cut in butter with pastry blender or two knives until mixture resembles fine crumbs. Press evenly into greased 13x9x2-inch baking pan. Bake 10 minutes. Pour topping (below) over cookie base; sprinkle with ½ cup pecans. Return to oven; bake 20 minutes. Cool completely; cut into 2x1-inch bars.

TOPPING: Melt Nestlé Milk Chocolate Morsels over hot (not boiling) water; remove from heat. In a small bowl, combine eggs, brown sugar, vanilla extract and salt; beat 2 minutes at high speed with electric mixer. Add melted chocolate; mix well. Stir in remaining ½ cup pecans.

Makes 4½ dozen 2x1-inch bars

# Chocolate Shortbread

## COOKIES

| | |
|---|---|
| 1 | 6-ounce package (1 cup) Nestlé Toll House Semi-Sweet Chocolate Morsels |
| 1¼ | cups sifted confectioners' sugar |
| ¾ | cup butter, softened |
| 1 | measuring teaspoon vanilla extract |
| 1 | cup all-purpose flour |
| ¼ | measuring teaspoon salt |
| 1 | cup ground nuts |

## CHOCOLATE GLAZE

| | |
|---|---|
| 1 | 6-ounce package (1 cup) Nestlé Toll House Semi-Sweet Chocolate Morsels |
| 2 | measuring tablespoons vegetable shortening |

COOKIES: Preheat oven to 250°F. Melt Nestlé Toll House Semi-Sweet Chocolate Morsels over hot (not boiling) water; remove from heat. In a large bowl, combine confectioners' sugar, butter and vanilla extract; beat until creamy. Gradually blend in flour and salt. Add melted chocolate and nuts; mix well. Shape into crescents, using 1 level measuring tablespoonful dough for each. Place on ungreased cookie sheets. Bake 30 minutes. Remove from cookie sheets; cool completely. Dip half of each crescent cookie into Chocolate Glaze (below). Place on waxed paper lined cookie sheets. Chill in refrigerator until chocolate sets (about 30 minutes).

CHOCOLATE GLAZE: Over hot (not boiling) water, combine Nestlé Toll House Semi-Sweet Chocolate Morsels and vegetable shortening; stir until morsels melt and mixture is smooth.

Makes 3 dozen crescent cookies

**PRESSED CHOCOLATE SHORTBREAD:** *After adding nuts, place dough in cookie press; force through desired disc onto ungreased cookie sheets. Proceed as directed.*

Makes about 6 dozen cookies

*Top and bottom: Butterscotch People. On Platters,*
*clockwise from top: Chocolate Dipped Shortbread Cookies,*
*Chocolate Shortbread, Milk Chocolate Pecan Bars*

43

# Chocolate-Dipped Shortbread Cookies

- **2** cups all-purpose flour
- **1** cup butter, softened
- **½** cup sifted confectioners' sugar
- **1** measuring teaspoon vanilla extract
- **1** 12-ounce package (2 cups) Nestlé Little Bits Semi-Sweet Chocolate, divided
- **1** measuring tablespoon vegetable shortening
- **¾** cup finely chopped nuts

Preheat over to 350°F. In a large bowl, combine flour, butter, confectioners' sugar and vanilla extract; mix until well blended. Stir in 1 cup Nestlé Little Bits Semi-Sweet Chocolate; mix well. Drop dough by rounded measuring teaspoonfuls onto ungreased cookie sheets; shape into 2-inch logs or press into circles using bottom of glass dipped in flour. Bake 10 to 12 minutes. Cool completely. Over hot (not boiling) water, melt remaining 1 cup Nestlé Little Bits Semi-Sweet Chocolate and shortening; remove from heat. Dip one end of each cookie into melted chocolate. Roll in nuts. Chill in refrigerator until firm (about 1 hour).

Makes 4½ dozen cookies

*Packing cookies for mailing: Select cookies that travel well. Soft, moist bar cookies, brownies and drop cookies are best; thin, crisp cookies crumble too easily. Avoid mailing cookies with fillings and frostings; they can become sticky during the trip. Select a sturdy packing container made of heavy cardboard or metal. Line it with plastic wrap, aluminum foil or waxed paper. Have an ample supply of filler available. Suitable fillers include crumpled aluminum foil, waxed paper, tissue paper, newspaper or paper towels. Place a layer of filler in the bottom of the container. Wrap cookies individually or back to back in aluminum foil or plastic wrap. If assorted cookies are used, place the heaviest ones on the bottom; arrange wrapped cookies neatly in rows, with filler between rows and layers. Place a filler layer on top. Tape container securely shut. Wrap in mailing paper and tie with string or use heavy-duty unbreakable wrapping tape. Mark box FRAGILE—HANDLE WITH CARE.*

# Butterscotch Thins

1 6-ounce package (1 cup) Nestlé Butterscotch Flavored Morsels
1/2 cup butter
2/3 cup firmly packed brown sugar
1 egg
1 1/3 cups all-purpose flour
3/4 measuring teaspoon baking soda
1/3 cup chopped nuts
3/4 measuring teaspoon vanilla extract

Over hot (not boiling) water, combine Nestlé Butterscotch Flavored Morsels and butter; stir until morsels melt and mixture is smooth. Transfer to a large bowl. Add brown sugar and egg; beat until light and fluffy. Add flour and baking soda. Stir in nuts and vanilla extract. Wrap in waxed paper; chill in refrigerator until firm enough to handle (about 1 hour). Shape into a log about 12x1 1/2 inches, wrap and return to refrigerator.

To bake, preheat oven to 375°F. Cut log into slices 1/8 inch thick. Place on ungreased cookie sheets. Bake 5 to 6 minutes.

Makes 8 dozen cookies

**BUTTERSCOTCH PEOPLE:** *Omit nuts. Prepare dough as directed and chill until firm enough to handle (about 1 hour). On a floured board or pastry cloth, roll out dough to 1/8-inch thickness. Cut out cookies, using an 8-inch gingerbread cookie cutter (or, if desired, a 2- to 2 1/2-inch cookie cutter. Bake 8-inch cookies for 7 to 9 minutes; bake 2- to 2 1/2-inch cookies 4 to 5 minutes. Outline cookies with your favorite glaze, if desired.*

Makes 9 8-inch cookies or about 6 dozen 2- to 2 1/2-inch cookies

# Chocolate Snappers

1¾ cups all-purpose flour
2 measuring teaspoons baking soda
1 measuring teaspoon cinnamon
¼ measuring teaspoon salt
¾ cup vegetable shortening
1 cup sugar
1 egg
¼ cup corn syrup
2 envelopes (2 ounces) Nestlé Choco-bake Unsweetened Baking Chocolate Flavor
Granulated sugar

Preheat oven to 350°F. In a small bowl, combine flour, baking soda, cinnamon and salt; set aside. In a large bowl, combine shortening. 1 cup sugar and egg; beat until creamy. Mix in corn syrup and Nestlé Choco-bake Unsweetened Baking Chocolate Flavor. Blend in flour mixture. Shape into balls, using 1 level measuring tablespoonful dough for each; roll in granulated sugar. Place on ungreased cookie sheet. Bake 15 minutes. Allow to stand a few minutes before removing from cookie sheets.

Makes 3 dozen 3-inch cookies

*CHOCO-MINT SNAPPERS:* Add ¼ measuring teaspoon peppermint extract along with corn syrup and Choco-bake.

*GIANT CHOCOLATE SNAPPERS:* Shape dough into balls, using ¼ cup dough for each cookie. Bake at 350°F. 18 to 20 minutes.

Makes 1 dozen 4- to 4½-inch cookies

# Magic Bars

½ cup butter
1½ cups graham cracker crumbs
1 14-ounce can sweetened condensed milk*
1 6-ounce package (1 cup) Nestlé Toll House Semi-Sweet Chocolate Morsels
1 3½-ounce can (1⅓ cups) flaked coconut
1 cup chopped nuts

Preheat oven to 350°F. (325°F. for glass dish). In 13x9x2-inch baking pan, melt butter in oven. Sprinkle crumbs over butter; mix together and press into pan. Pour sweetened condensed milk evenly over crumbs. Top evenly with remaining ingredients; press down firmly. Bake 25 to 30 minutes or until lightly browned. Cool thoroughly before cutting. Store loosely covered at room temperature.

Makes 24 bars

*Not evaporated milk

# *Chocolate Sandwich Cookies*

|       |                                          |
|-------|------------------------------------------|
| 2     | cups all-purpose flour                   |
| 1½    | measuring teaspoons baking powder        |
| ½     | measuring teaspoon baking soda           |
| ½     | measuring teaspoon salt                  |
| ½     | cup butter, softened                     |
| 1¼    | cups sugar                               |
| 1     | measuring teaspoon vanilla extract       |
| 3     | envelopes (3 ounces) Nestlé Choco-bake Unsweetened Baking Chocolate Flavor |
| 2     | eggs                                     |
|       | Peanut butter or frosting                |

In a small bowl, combine flour, baking powder, baking soda and salt; set aside. In a large bowl, combine butter, sugar and vanilla extract; beat until creamy. Blend in Nestlé Choco-bake Unsweetened Baking Chocolate Flavor. Beat in eggs. Gradually add flour mixture; mix well. Divide dough in half. Shape each half into a ball and wrap with waxed paper. Chill in refrigerator about 1 hour.

Preheat oven to 350°F. On a lightly floured board or pastry cloth, roll out dough to ⅛ inch thickness. Cut with a 2½-inch round cookie cutter. Place on ungreased cookie sheets. Bake 8 to 10 minutes. Cool completely. For each sandwich cookie, spread 1 cooled wafer with peanut butter or your favorite frosting; top with another.

Makes 3 dozen 2½-inch sandwich cookies

# Oatmeal Scotchies

1 cup all-purpose flour
1 measuring teaspoon baking soda
½ measuring teaspoon salt
½ measuring teaspoon cinnamon
1 cup butter or margarine, softened
¾ cup sugar
¾ cup firmly packed brown sugar
2 eggs
1 measuring teaspoon vanilla extract
3 cups oats (quick or old-fashioned), uncooked
1 12-ounce package (2 cups) Nestlé Butterscotch Flavored
   Morsels

Preheat oven to 375°F. In a small bowl, combine flour, baking soda, salt and cinnamon; set aside. In a large bowl, combine butter, sugar, brown sugar, eggs and vanilla extract; beat until light and fluffy. Gradually add flour mixture. Stir in oats and Nestlé Butterscotch Flavored Morsels. Drop by level measuring tablespoons onto ungreased cookie sheets. Bake 7 to 8 minutes for chewier cookies or 9 to 10 minutes for crisper cookies.

Makes about 4 dozen 3-inch cookies.

# Oatmeal Marble Squares

¾ cup all-purpose flour
½ measuring teaspoon baking soda
½ measuring teaspoon salt
½ cup butter, softened
6 measuring tablespoons sugar
6 measuring tablespoons firmly packed brown sugar
½ measuring teaspoon vanilla extract
1 egg
1 cup quick oats, uncooked
½ cup chopped nuts
1 6-ounce package (1 cup) Nestlé Toll House Semi-Sweet
   Chocolate Morsels

Preheat oven to 375°F. In a small bowl, combine flour, baking soda and salt; set aside. In a large bowl, combine butter, sugar, brown sugar and vanilla extract; beat until creamy. Beat in egg. Blend in flour mixture. Stir in oats and nuts. Spread into greased 13x9x2-inch baking pan. Sprinkle Nestlé Toll House Semi-Sweet Chocolate Morsels over top. Place in oven for 3 minutes. Run knife through to marbleize. Bake 10 to 12 minutes. Cool; cut into 2-inch squares.

Makes 2 dozen 2-inch squares

*From top: Oatmeal Marble Squares,
Fudge Drops, Oatmeal Scotchies*

49

# Double Peanut Butter Brownies

1    cup all-purpose flour
1    measuring teaspoon baking powder
1    measuring teaspoon salt
1    12-ounce package (2 cups) Nestlé Peanut Butter
     Morsels, divided
1/3   cup butter
1/2   cup firmly packed brown sugar
1/2   cup sugar
2    eggs
1/2   measuring teaspoon vanilla extract

Preheat oven to 350°F. In a small bowl, combine flour, baking powder and salt; set aside. Over hot (not boiling) water, combine 1 cup Nestlé Peanut Butter Morsels and butter; heat until morsels melt and mixture is smooth. Transfer to a large bowl. Stir in brown sugar and sugar. Beat in eggs and vanilla extract. Blend in flour mixture. Stir in remaining 1 cup Nestlé Peanut Butter Morsels. Spread evenly into greased 9-inch square pan. Bake 30 to 35 minutes. Cool completely. Cut into 1½-inch squares.

Makes 36 1½-inch squares

# Chocolate Crispies

1    cup all-purpose flour
1/2   measuring teaspoon baking powder
1/2   measuring teaspoon baking soda
1/2   measuring teaspoon salt
1/2   cup butter, softened
1/2   cup firmly packed brown sugar
1/2   cup sugar
1    egg
2    envelopes (2 ounces) Nestlé Choco-bake Unsweetened Baking
     Chocolate Flavor
1/2   cup quick oats, uncooked
1/2   cup shredded coconut

Preheat oven to 350°F. In a small bowl, combine flour, baking powder, baking soda and salt; set aside. In a large bowl, combine butter, brown sugar, sugar and egg; beat until creamy. Blend in Nestlé Choco-bake Unsweetened Baking Chocolate Flavor. Add flour mixture, oats and coconut; mix until well blended. Drop by rounded measuring teaspoonfuls onto greased cookie sheets. Bake 10 to 12 minutes.

Makes 3 dozen 2-inch cookies

# Mix 'Ems

Mix together in a plastic bag or container one (or more) of the following combinations:

1 6-ounce package (1 cup) Nestlé Toll House Semi-Sweet
   Chocolate Morsels or Nestlé Butterscotch Flavored Morsels
1 cup salted peanuts
1 cup raisins

1 6-ounce package (1 cup) Nestlé Toll House Semi-Sweet
   Chocolate Morsels or Nestlé Butterscotch Flavored Morsels
1 cup potato sticks
1 cup coarsely broken pretzel sticks

1 6-ounce package (1 cup) Nestlé Toll House Semi-Sweet
   Chocolate Morsels or Nestlé Butterscotch Flavored Morsels
1 cup coarsely broken peanut brittle
1 cup raisins

1 6-ounce package (1 cup) Nestlé Toll House Semi-Sweet
   Chocolate Morsels or Nestlé Butterscotch Flavored Morsels
1 6-ounce package (1 cup) Nestlé Butterscotch Flavored Morsels
1 cup broken corn chips

1 6-ounce package (1 cup) Nestlé Toll House Semi-Sweet
   Chocolate Morsels or Nestlé Butterscotch Flavored Morsels
1 cup ready-to-eat cereal
1 cup raisins

1 6-ounce package (1 cup) Nestlé Toll House Semi-Sweet
   Chocolate Morsels or Nestlé Butterscotch Flavored Morsels
1 8-ounce package ($1\frac{1}{2}$ cups) chopped dates
1 cup salted cashews

1 12-ounce package (2 cups) Nestlé Peanut Butter Morsels
2 cups broken graham crackers (about 6 crackers)
1 cup raisins
1 cup coconut

1 12-ounce package (2 cups) Nestlé Peanut Butter Morsels
2 cups bite-size shredded rice biscuits
1 cup raisins

1 12-ounce package (2 cups) Nestlé Peanut Butter Morsels
1 12-ounce package (2 cups) Nestlé Milk Chocolate Morsels

# Coconut Creams

3    measuring tablespoons butter, softened
3    measuring tablespoons corn syrup
1    measuring teaspoon vanilla extract
¼    measuring teaspoon salt
2½   cups sifted confectioners' sugar
1    3½-ounce can shredded coconut, chopped
1    11½-ounce package (2 cups) Nestlé Milk Chocolate Morsels
1    measuring tablespoon vegetable shortening

In a small bowl, combine butter, corn syrup, vanilla extract and salt. Gradually add confectioners' sugar; beat well. Mixture will be crumbly. Add coconut; knead mixture until smooth and pliable. Roll into 1-inch balls; freeze 10 minutes. Over hot (not boiling) water, combine Nestlé Milk Chocolate Morsels and vegetable shortening; heat until morsels melt and mixture is smooth. Remove from heat, but keep over hot water. Dip coconut balls into melted chocolate; shake off excess chocolate. Place on waxed paper-lined cookie sheets. Chill until firm (about 20 to 30 minutes). Store in refrigerator until ready to serve.

Makes about 30 1-inch balls

**PEPPERMINT CREAMS:** *Omit coconut. Add 1 to 2 measuring table-spoons crushed peppermint candy when kneading mixture. Dip as above. Place on waxed paper-lined cookie sheets. Sprinkle tops with crushed peppermint candy. Chill until firm (about 20 to 30 minutes). Serve immediately or store in refrigerator until ready to serve.*

# Apple Cartwheels

**8**   medium-size apples
**1**   6-ounce package (1 cup) Nestlé Toll House Semi-Sweet
        Chocolate Morsels
**½**   cup peanut butter
**¼**   cup raisins
**1**   measuring tablespoon honey

Remove core from each apple, leaving a cavity 1¼ inches in diameter. Set aside. In blender container, process Nestlé Toll House Semi-Sweet Chocolate Morsels 5 seconds or until morsels are chopped. In a small bowl, mix chopped chocolate, peanut butter, raisins and honey. Stuff cored apples with chocolate-peanut butter filling. Wrap each apple with plastic wrap. Chill in refrigerator. When ready to serve, slice crosswise in ½-inch slices.

Makes 32 cartwheels

# Blueberry Clusters

**1**    11½-ounce package (2 cups) Nestlé Milk Chocolate Morsels
**¼**    cup vegetable shortening
**36**   1¼-inch candy liners
**2**    cups fresh blueberries, washed and dried

Over hot (not boiling) water, combine Nestlé Milk Chocolate Morsels and shortening; stir until morsels melt and mixture is smooth. Remove from heat. Place 1 measuring teaspoonful of melted chocolate in candy liner; add 6 to 8 blueberries. Top with additional 2 measuring teaspoonfuls of chocolate, making sure blueberries are well coated. Chill in refrigerator until chocolate is set (20 to 30 minutes). Store in refrigerator until ready to serve.

Makes about 2½ dozen clusters

*Note:* Blueberry clusters may be kept at room temperature up to 1 hour.
If chocolate becomes sticky, return to refrigerator.

# Milk Chocolate Pralines

3   cups sugar
¾   cup water
¼   cup light corn syrup
1   measuring teaspoon vinegar
½   measuring teaspoon salt
1   11½-ounce package (2 cups) Nestlé Milk Chocolate Morsels
1   cup coarsely chopped pecans
    Pecan halves (optional)

In a large saucepan, combine sugar, water, corn syrup, vinegar and salt. Bring to *full boil*, stirring constantly. Boil 3 minutes *without stirring*. Remove from heat; cool 5 minutes. Add Nestlé Milk Chocolate Morsels; stir quickly until melted. Stir in pecans. Quickly drop by level measuring tablespoonfuls onto foil-lined cookie sheets.* Garnish with pecan halves, if desired. Refrigerate until set (about 20 minutes). Peel candies off foil to serve. Store in refrigerator.

Makes 4 dozen 2-inch candies

*Work as rapidly as possible as mixture tends to set up quickly.

# Peanut Butter Burst Cookies

2   cups all-purpose flour
1   measuring teaspoon baking powder
¼   measuring teaspoon salt
1   cup butter, softened
¾   cup firmly packed brown sugar
½   cup sugar
½   measuring teaspoon vanilla extract
1   egg
1   12-ounce package (2 cups) Nestlé Peanut Butter Morsels

Preheat oven to 375°F. In a small bowl, combine flour, baking powder and salt; set aside. In a large bowl, combine butter, brown sugar, sugar and vanilla extract; beat at medium speed until creamy (about 3 to 5 minutes). Add egg; beat well. Turn mixer to low. Gradually add flour mixture. Stir in Nestlé Peanut Butter Morsels. Drop by rounded measuring teaspoonfuls onto ungreased cookie sheets. Bake 7 to 9 minutes. Let cool 2 minutes before removing from cookie sheets; cool completely. Cookies will be pale in color with a light brown edge.

Makes 6 dozen 2-inch cookies

# *Dipped Fruit Balls*

2   8-ounce packages pitted dates
2   cups dried apricots
1   11½-ounce package (2 cups) Nestlé Milk Chocolate Morsels
2   measuring tablespoons vegetable shortening
    Paper candy liners

Finely chop dates and apricots; mix well. Over hot (not boiling) water, melt Nestlé Milk Chocolate Morsels and vegetable shortening, remove from heat, but keep over hot water. With greased hands, shape date-apricot mixture into 1-inch balls. Dip the balls into melted chocolate mixture. Place on foil-lined cookie sheets. Refrigerate until ready to serve (about 15 to 20 minutes).

Makes about 3 dozen candies

*Peanut Butter Burst Cookies,*
*Peanut Butter Jelly Bars*

# Peanut Butter Jelly Bars

2   cups all-purpose flour
1/2   measuring teaspoon salt
1/2   cup butter, softened
1/2   cup sugar
1   12-ounce package (2 cups) Nestlé Peanut Butter Morsels, divided
1   cup red currant jelly

Preheat oven to 375°F. In a small bowl, combine flour and salt; set aside. In a large bowl, combine butter and sugar; beat until creamy. Gradually add flour mixture; beat until mixture forms fine crumbs. Reserve 1 cup crumb mixture; set aside. Press remaining mixture into greased 9x13x2-inch baking pan. Bake 10 minutes.

In a small bowl, combine 1½ cups Nestlé Peanut Butter Morsels and red currant jelly. Spread over baked base. Melt over hot (not boiling) water remaining ½ cup Nestlé Peanut Butter Morsels. Remove from heat. Stir in reserved crumb mixture. Sprinkle over peanut butter–jelly layer. Bake 15 to 18 minutes. Cool completely; cut into 2x1-inch bars.

Makes 4½ dozen 2x1-inch bars

# Peanut Butter-Granola Cookies

2   cups all-purpose flour
2   measuring teaspoons baking powder
1   measuring teaspoon baking soda
1   measuring teaspoon salt
1   cup butter, softened
1½   cups firmly packed brown sugar
2   eggs
1   measuring tablespoon water
1½   cups natural cereal
1   12-ounce package (2 cups) Nestlé Peanut Butter Morsels

Preheat oven to 375°F. In a small bowl, combine flour, baking powder, baking soda and salt; set aside. In a large bowl, combine butter, brown sugar, eggs and water; beat until creamy. Gradually add flour mixture. Stir in natural cereal and Nestlé Peanut Butter Morsels. Drop by rounded measuring teaspoonfuls onto ungreased cookie sheets. Bake 8 to 10 minutes.

Makes 8 dozen 2-inch cookies

# *Little Bits Cream Puffs*

**PUFFS**

- ½   **cup butter**
- 1   **cup water**
- 1   **cup all-purpose flour**
- ¼   **measuring teaspoon salt**
- 4   **eggs**
- 1½   **measuring tablespoons sugar**
- ½   **measuring teaspoon grated lemon rind**
- 1   **measuring tablespoon vanilla extract**

**LITTLE BITS FILLING**

- 2   **cups ricotta cheese**
- ¼   **cup plus 2 measuring tablespoons sugar**
- 1   **measuring teaspoon lemon extract**
- 2   **measuring tablespoons orange liqueur***
- 1   **cup heavy cream, whipped**
- ½   **of 12-ounce package (1 cup) Nestlé Little Bits Semi-Sweet Chocolate**

Preheat oven to 400°F. In a medium saucepan, combine butter and water. Bring *just to a boil;* remove from heat. Add flour and salt at once; beat vigorously with wooden spoon. Return to heat; beat until mixture forms ball. Remove from heat; cool slightly. Add eggs, one at a time, beating well by hand after each addition. Stir in sugar, lemon rind and vanilla extract. Drop by rounded measuring teaspoonfuls (for bite-size puffs) or by rounded measuring tablespoonfuls (for dessert puffs) onto greased cookie sheets. Bake 10 minutes. Reduce oven temperature to 350°F. Bake 15 minutes (for bite-size puffs) or 20 minutes (for dessert puffs). Remove from oven; split. Cool and fill with Little Bits Filling (below).

LITTLE BITS FILLING: In a large bowl, combine ricotta cheese, sugar, lemon extract and orange liqueur; beat until smooth. Fold in whipped cream. Stir in Nestlé Little Bits Semi-Sweet Chocolate. Fill cooled cream puff shells.

Makes 36 bite-size puffs or 15 dessert puffs

*½ measuring tablespoon lemon rind plus 1 measuring tablespoon lemon extract can be substituted for orange liqueur, if desired.

*Little Bits Cream Puffs*

# *Peanut Fudge Log*

½    cup chunky peanut butter
1    measuring tablespoon butter or margarine, softened
2    measuring tablespoons sifted confectioners' sugar
1    measuring tablespoon orange juice
1    measuring teaspoon orange rind
1    measuring teaspoon vanilla extract
½    cup chopped nuts
½    cup chopped raisins
1    11½-ounce package (2 cups) Nestlé Milk Chocolate Morsels
½    cup sweetened condensed milk*
⅛    measuring teaspoon salt
½    measuring teaspoon vanilla extract

In a small bowl, combine peanut butter, butter or margarine, confectioners' sugar, orange juice, orange rind and 1 measuring teaspoon vanilla extract. Beat until well blended. Add nuts and raisins; mix well. Roll into two 10-inch logs; set aside. Over hot (not boiling) water, combine Nestlé Milk Chocolate Morsels, sweetened condensed milk and salt; heat until morsels melt and mixture is smooth. Remove from heat; add ½ measuring teaspoon vanilla extract. Pat half of mixture into 10x3½-inch oblong. Place 1 log in center of oblong; roll up and seal seam. Take remaining half of mixture and repeat for second log. Wrap in waxed paper. Chill until firm (about 1 hour). Cut into ¼-inch slices.

Makes 80 candies

*Not evaporated milk

*Note:* Logs may be frozen up to 1 month.

# Chocolate–Peanut Butter Brownies

1⅓   cups all-purpose flour
1   measuring teaspoon baking powder
1   measuring teaspoon salt
2   cups sugar
⅔   cup butter, softened
4   eggs
2   envelopes (2 ounces) Nestlé Choco-bake Unsweetened Baking Chocolate Flavor
1   measuring teaspoon vanilla extract
1   12-ounce package (2 cups) Nestlé Peanut Butter Morsels

Preheat oven to 350°F. In a small bowl, combine flour, baking powder and salt; set aside. In a large bowl, combine sugar, butter, eggs. Nestlé Choco-bake Unsweetened Baking Chocolate Flavor and vanilla extract; beat until creamy. Gradually add flour mixture; mix well. Stir in Nestlé Peanut Butter Morsels. Spread in greased 13x9x2-inch baking pan. Bake 30 to 35 minutes. Cool completely. Cut into 1½-inch squares.

Makes 48 1½-inch squares

# *Chocolate Clusters*

1   11½-ounce package (2 cups) Nestlé Milk Chocolate Morsels
1   measuring tablespoon vegetable shortening
⅓   cup miniature marshmallows
⅓   cup peanuts, salted or unsalted
⅓   cup raisins
24   1¼-inch foil candy liners

Over hot (not boiling) water, combine Nestlé Milk Chocolate Morsels and vegetable shortening; stir until morsels melt and mixture is smooth. Keep over low heat. In a small bowl, combine marshmallows, peanuts and raisins. Fill candy liners halfway with nut mixture (about 1 measuring teaspoonful); place on a cookie sheet. Spoon 2 measuring teaspoonfuls melted chocolate on top of nut mixture; spread to seal completely. Chill until firm (about 30 minutes). Serve immediately or store in refrigerator until ready to serve.

Makes 24 candies

# Cakes and Breads

When we think back to Grandma, it is her graciousness that we recall. How, despite the batters to beat by hand, the stove to stoke, the water to heat for washing up, the food appeared as if by magic.

What pleasure to munch warm, fragrant coffeecake and exchange family news with your next-door neighbor, how good to share a glass of cider and a doughnut with the kids on a sparkling autumn afternoon and what fun to bake a super-special layer cake and invite friends for after-dinner coffee and dessert.

That's the way Grandma lived. With these heritage recipes, you can preserve that gracious aura, creating islands of tranquility in the midst of your busy and demanding life.

# Chocolate Layer Cake

2¼ cups all-purpose flour
1½ measuring teaspoons baking soda
1 measuring teaspoon salt
½ cup butter, softened
1½ cups sugar
1 measuring teaspoon vanilla extract
2 envelopes (2 ounces) Nestlé Choco-bake Unsweetened Baking Chocolate Flavor
2 eggs
1½ cups ice water
Sour Cream Velvet Frosting (optional)

Preheat oven to 350°F. In a small bowl, combine flour, baking soda and salt; set aside. In a large bowl, combine butter, sugar and vanilla extract; beat until creamy. Blend in Nestlé Choco-bake Unsweetened Baking Chocolate Flavor. Add eggs, one at a time, beating well after each addition. Blend in flour mixture alternately with ice water. Pour into two greased and floured 8- or 9-inch round cake pans. Bake 30 to 35 minutes. Cool 10 minutes; remove from pans. Cool completely on wire racks. Frost with Sour Cream Velvet Frosting (page 124) or favorite frosting, if desired.

Makes 2 8- or 9-inch cake layers

# Brown Sugar Fudge Cake

1¾ cups all-purpose flour
1 measuring teaspoon baking soda
¾ measuring teaspoon salt
½ cup butter, softened
1½ cups firmly packed brown sugar
1 measuring teaspoon vanilla extract
3 eggs
3 envelopes (3 ounces) Nestlé Choco-bake Unsweetened Baking Chocolate Flavor
1 cup buttermilk

Preheat oven to 350°F. In a small bowl, combine flour, baking soda and salt; set aside. In a large bowl, combine butter, brown sugar and vanilla extract; beat until creamy. Add eggs, one at a time, beating well after each addition. Blend in Nestlé Choco-bake Unsweetened Baking Chocolate Flavor. Add flour mixture alternately with buttermilk. Pour batter into two greased and floured 9-inch round cake pans. Bake 30 to 35 minutes. Cool 10 minutes; remove from pans. Cool completely on wire racks. Fill and frost with your favorite frosting.

Makes two 9-inch cake layers

*Chocolate Layer Cake frosted with
Sour Cream Velvet Frosting*

# *Sachertorte*

## CAKE

1    6-ounce package (1 cup) Nestlé Toll House Semi-Sweet Chocolate Morsels
1¼   cups water
1¾   cups all-purpose flour
1½   measuring teaspoons baking soda
1    measuring teaspoon salt
6    eggs
1    measuring teaspoon vanilla extract
1½   cups sugar
1    12-ounce jar apricot preserves, divided

## CHOCOLATE GLAZE

½   cup evaporated milk
    Dash salt
1   6-ounce package (1 cup) Nestlé Toll House Semi-Sweet Chocolate Morsels

CAKE: Preheat oven to 350°F. Over hot (not boiling) water, combine 6-ounces (1 cup) Nestlé Toll House Semi-Sweet Chocolate Morsels and the water; heat until morsels melt and mixture is smooth. Remove from heat; set aside. In a small bowl, combine flour, baking soda and salt; set aside. In a large bowl, beat eggs and vanilla extract until foamy. Gradually add sugar, beating until thick and lemon colored, about 5 minutes. Gradually add flour mixture alternately with chocolate mixture. Pour batter into three well-greased and floured 9-inch round pans. Bake 25 minutes. Loosen edges of cakes from pans. Remove from pans; cool completely. Spread ½ jar preserves over one cake layer. Place second layer on top; spread with remaining ½ jar preserves. Top with plain layer. Spread top and sides of cake with Chocolate Glaze (below).

CHOCOLATE GLAZE: In a small saucepan, combine evaporated milk and salt. Bring *just to a boil* over moderate heat. Remove from heat. Add 6-ounces (1 cup) Nestlé Toll House Semi-Sweet Chocolate Morsels; stir until morsels melt and mixture is smooth.

Makes one 9-inch layer cake and 1 cup glaze

# Chocolate-Vanilla Swirl Cake

1    12-ounce package (2 cups) Nestlé Toll House Semi-Sweet
     Chocolate Morsels
2½   cups all-purpose flour
2    measuring teaspoons baking powder
½    measuring teaspoon salt
1    cup butter, softened
1½   cups sugar
4    eggs
1    measuring tablespoon vanilla extract
1    cup milk
1    cup chopped pecans
     Confectioners' sugar

Preheat oven to 375°F. Melt Nestlé Toll House Semi-Sweet Chocolate Morsels over hot (not boiling) water; remove from heat and cool. In a small bowl, combine flour, baking powder and salt; set aside. In a large bowl, combine butter and sugar; beat until creamy. Add eggs, one at a time, beating well after each addition; beat in vanilla extract. Gradually blend in flour mixture alternately with milk. Divide batter in half. Stir melted chocolate into one half and chopped pecans into the other. Alternately layer batters into greased 10-inch fluted or plain tube pan. Bake 60 to 70 minutes. Cool 10 minutes and remove from pan. Dust top with confectioners' sugar.

Makes one 10-inch ring cake

*Frost the cake and not the plate:* Before placing unfrosted cake, or bottom cake layer, on the serving plate, overlap three or four pieces of waxed paper around the edges of the plate. (If you use a paper doily, cover it with the waxed paper.) Place cake or cake layer on top. Leave the waxed paper until you've completely finished frosting and decorating, then carefully remove the sheets — and admire your masterpiece.

*Black Forest Cherry Torte, Sachertorte*

# Black Forest Cherry Torte

**CAKE**

- 1   12-ounce package (2 cups) Nestlé Toll House Semi-Sweet Chocolate Morsels
- ½   cup milk
- 2   measuring tablespoons sugar
- 1¾   cups all-purpose flour
- 1   measuring teaspoon baking soda
- 1   measuring teaspoon salt
- ¼   cup butter, softened
- ⅔   cup sugar
- 3   eggs
- ⅔   cup milk
- 1   measuring teaspoon vanilla extract
- ¼   cup brandy, divided
- 1   21-ounce can (2 cups) cherry pie filling, divided

**BRANDIED WHIPPED CREAM**

- 2   cups heavy cream, whipped
- 3   measuring tablespoons brandy
- ⅓   cup sifted confectioners' sugar

CAKE: Preheat oven to 350°F. Over hot (not boiling) water, combine Nestlé Toll House Semi-Sweet Chocolate Morsels, ½ cup milk and 2 measuring tablespoons sugar. Stir until morsels melt and mixture is smooth; set aside. In a small bowl, combine flour, baking soda and salt; set aside. In a large bowl, combine butter and ⅔ cup sugar; beat until creamy. Add eggs, one at a time, beating well after each addition. Blend in flour mixture alternately with ⅔ cup milk. Stir in chocolate mixture and vanilla extract. Pour evenly into two well-greased and floured 8- or 9-inch cake pans. Bake 25 to 30 minutes. Cool 10 minutes. Remove from pans; cool completely. Using a long, thin serrated knife, slice each layer in half crosswise and sprinkle each with 1 measuring tablespoon brandy. Spread 1 cup Brandied Whipped Cream (below) on one layer. Spread about ⅔ cup cherry pie filling over whipped cream ½ inch from edge. Repeat with next two layers. Place last layer on top; spread with remaining whipped cream. Garnish with Chocolate Curls (page 113), if desired.

BRANDIED WHIPPED CREAM: In a large bowl, beat heavy cream. Gradually add brandy and confectioners' sugar, beating until soft peaks form.

Makes one 8- or 9-inch torte

# Chocolate Cheesecake

**CAKE**

- 1   cup graham cracker crumbs
- 3   measuring tablespoons sugar
- 3   measuring tablespoons butter, melted
- 1   12-ounce package (2 cups) Nestlé Toll House Semi-Sweet Chocolate Morsels
- 2   8-ounce packages cream cheese, softened
- 2   eggs
- ¾   cup sugar
- 2   measuring tablespoons all-purpose flour
- 1   measuring teaspoon vanilla extract

**GARNISH**

- ½   cup heavy cream, whipped
- Sliced strawberries

CAKE: Preheat oven to 350°F. In a small bowl, combine graham cracker crumbs, sugar and butter; mix well. Press into bottom of a 9-inch springform pan. Melt Nestlé Toll House Semi-Sweet Chocolate Morsels over hot (not boiling) water; remove from heat. In a large bowl, beat cream cheese until creamy. Beat in eggs, sugar, flour and vanilla extract. Blend in melted chocolate. Pour into crumb-lined pan. Bake 1 hour 15 minutes. Cool cheesecake completely before removing rim.

GARNISH: Spread top of cake evenly with whipped cream. Decorate with sliced strawberries. Chill in refrigerator until ready to serve.

Makes one 9-inch cheesecake

# Little Bits Cheesecake

- 1¼   cups graham cracker crumbs
- 2   measuring tablespoons sugar
- ¼   cup butter, melted
- 2   8-ounce packages cream cheese, softened
- ¾   cup sugar
- ½   cup sour cream
- 1   measuring tablespoon vanilla extract
- 4   eggs
- ½   of 12-ounce package (1 cup) Nestlé Little Bits Semi-Sweet Chocolate

Preheat oven to 325°F. In a small bowl, combine graham cracker crumbs, 2 measuring tablespoons sugar and butter; mix well. Pat firmly into a 9-inch springform pan, covering bottom and 1 inch up sides; set aside. In a large bowl, beat cream cheese until light and creamy. Gradually beat in ¾ cup sugar. Mix in sour cream and vanilla extract. Add eggs, one at a time, beating well after each addition. Pour half the batter into crumb-lined pan; sprinkle with ½ cup Nestlé Little Bits Semi-Sweet Chocolate. Pour remaining batter on top; sprinkle with remaining ½ cup Nestlé Little Bits Semi-Sweet Chocolate. Place in shallow pan filled with about 1 inch water.* Bake 50 to 55 minutes or until only a 2- or 3-inch circle in center will shake. Cool at room temperature; refrigerate until ready to serve.

Makes one 9-inch cheesecake

*If springform pan does not clip together securely, wrap bottom with aluminum foil to prevent water from seeping in during baking.

## *Chocolate Swirl Cheesecake*

|     |                                                                          |
|-----|--------------------------------------------------------------------------|
| 1   | 6-ounce package (1 cup) Nestlé Toll House Semi-Sweet Chocolate Morsels    |
| ½   | cup sugar                                                                |
| 1¼  | cups graham cracker crumbs                                               |
| 2   | measuring tablespoons sugar                                              |
| ¼   | cup butter, melted                                                       |
| 2   | 8-ounce packages cream cheese, softened                                  |
| ¾   | cup sugar                                                                |
| ½   | cup sour cream                                                           |
| 1   | measuring teaspoon vanilla extract                                       |
| 4   | eggs                                                                     |

Preheat oven to 325°F. Over hot (not boiling) water, combine Nestlé Toll House Semi-Sweet Chocolate Morsels and ½ cup sugar; heat until morsels melt and mixture is smooth. Remove from heat; set aside. In a small bowl, combine graham cracker crumbs, 2 measuring tablespoons sugar and the butter; mix well. Pat firmly into a 9-inch springform pan, covering bottom and 1 inch up sides; set aside. In a large bowl, beat cream cheese until light and creamy. Gradually beat in ¾ cup sugar. Mix in sour cream and vanilla extract. Add eggs, one at a time, beating well after each addition. Divide batter in half. Stir melted chocolate mixture into one half. Pour into crumb-lined pan; cover with plain batter. With a knife, swirl chocolate batter through plain batter to marbleize. Bake 50 minutes or until only a 2- to 3-inch circle in center will shake. Cool at room temperature; refrigerate until ready to serve.

Makes one 9-inch cheesecake

*Chocolate Cheesecake,*
*Chocolate Swirl Cheesecake*

# *Fudge Ribbon Cake*

## RIBBON LAYER

- **1** **8-ounce package cream cheese, softened**
- **¼** **cup sugar**
- **2** **measuring tablespoons butter**
- **1** **measuring tablespoon cornstarch**
- **1** **egg**
- **2** **measuring tablespoons milk**
- **½** **measuring teaspoon vanilla extract**

## CAKE

- **2** **cups all-purpose flour**
- **1** **measuring teaspoon baking powder**
- **½** **measuring teaspoon baking soda**
- **½** **cup butter, softened**
- **2** **cups sugar**
- **1** **measuring teaspoon vanilla extract**
- **2** **eggs**
- **1⅓** **cups milk**
- **4** **envelopes (4 ounces) Nestlé Choco-bake Unsweetened Baking Chocolate Flavor**

## CHOCOLATE FROSTING

- **¼** **cup milk**
- **¼** **cup butter**
- **2** **envelopes (2 ounces) Nestlé Choco-bake Unsweetened Baking Chocolate Flavor**
- **1** **measuring teaspoon vanilla extract**
- **2½** **cups sifted confectioners' sugar**

RIBBON LAYER: Preheat oven to 350°F. In a small bowl, combine cream cheese, sugar, butter and cornstarch; beat until creamy. Add egg, milk and vanilla extract; beat until well blended and smooth.

CAKE: In a small bowl, combine flour, baking powder and baking soda; set aside. In a large bowl, combine butter, sugar and vanilla extract; mix well. Beat in eggs. Add flour mixture alternately with milk. Blend in Nestlé Choco-bake Unsweetened Baking Chocolate Flavor; mix well. Pour half the batter into a greased and floured 13x9x2-inch baking pan. Spoon ribbon layer mixture over batter; spread to cover. Top with remaining batter. Bake 50 to 60 minutes. Cool cake in pan. Frost with Chocolate Frosting (below).

CHOCOLATE FROSTING: In a large saucepan, combine milk and butter. Bring to boil; remove from heat. Blend in Nestlé Choco-bake Unsweetened Chocolate Flavor and vanilla extract. Stir in confectioners' sugar; blend until smooth. Thin with a few drops milk, if necessary.

Makes one frosted 13x9x2-inch cake

# Sherry Fruitcake

- 2 cups chopped dates
- 2 cups chopped pecans
- 2 cups whole candied cherries
- 1 cup mixed candied fruit
- 1 12-ounce package (2 cups) Nestlé Toll House Semi-Sweet Chocolate Morsels
- ½ cup cream sherry
- 6 eggs
- 1 cup sugar
- 2 measuring teaspoons vanilla extract
- 3 cups all-purpose flour
- 2 measuring teaspoons salt

In a large bowl, combine dates, pecans, candied cherries, candied fruit and Nestlé Toll House Semi-Sweet Chocolate Morsels; add sherry and let stand 1 hour, stirring occasionally. Preheat oven to 325°F. In a large bowl, beat eggs until thick and lemon colored (about 5 minutes). Gradually beat in sugar and vanilla extract. Combine flour and salt; mix with fruit mixture. Fold in egg mixture. Spread into greased and floured 9-inch tube pan. Bake 1 hour. Cool in pan 15 minutes. Remove cake from pan; cool completely on wire rack.

Makes one 9-inch fruitcake

# Butterscotch Banana Bread

- 3½ cups all-purpose flour
- 4 measuring teaspoons baking powder
- 1 measuring teaspoon baking soda
- 1 measuring teaspoon cinnamon
- 1 measuring teaspoon nutmeg
- 1 measuring teaspoon salt
- 2 cups ripe mashed bananas (4 to 6 medium bananas)
- 1½ cups sugar
- 2 eggs
- ½ cup butter, melted
- ½ cup milk
- 2⅔ cups chopped pecans, divided
- 1 12-ounce package (2 cups) Nestlé Butterscotch Flavored Morsels

Preheat oven to 350°F. In a small bowl, combine flour, baking powder, baking soda, cinnamon, nutmeg and salt; set aside. In a large bowl, combine bananas, sugar, eggs, and butter; beat until creamy. Gradually add flour mixture alternately with milk; mix until well blended. Stir in 2 cups pecans and the Nestlé Butterscotch Morsels. Pour batter equally into two well-greased and floured

9x5x3-inch loaf pans. Sprinkle tops equally with remaining ⅔ cup pecans. Bake 60 to 70 minutes. Cool 15 minutes; remove from pans.

Makes 2 loaves

*Note:* To make 1 loaf, divide ingredients in half.

# *Rich Devil's Food Cake*

## CAKE

| | |
|---|---|
| 1¼ | cups all-purpose flour |
| 1 | measuring teaspoon baking soda |
| 1 | measuring teaspoon salt |
| ½ | cup butter, softened |
| 1¼ | cups sugar |
| 3 | envelopes (3 ounces) Nestlé Choco-bake Unsweetened Baking Chocolate Flavor |
| 1 | measuring teaspoon vanilla extract |
| 2 | eggs |
| 1 | cup milk |
| ⅛ | measuring teaspoon red food coloring (optional) |

## CHOCOLATY CREAM FROSTING

| | |
|---|---|
| 3½ | cups sifted confectioners' sugar, divided |
| ½ | cup butter, softened |
| 3 | envelopes (3 ounces) Nestlé Choco-bake Unsweetened Baking Chocolate Flavor |
| 1 | measuring teaspoon vanilla extract |
| ⅛ | measuring teaspoon salt |
| 1 | egg |
| ¼ | cup milk |

CAKE: Preheat oven to 350°F. In a small bowl, combine flour, baking soda and salt; set aside. In large bowl, combine butter and sugar; beat until creamy. Blend in Nestlé Choco-bake Unsweetened Baking Chocolate Flavor and vanilla extract. Add eggs, one at a time, beating well after each addition. Blend in flour mixture alternately with milk. Stir in food coloring. Pour into two well-greased and floured 8- or 9-inch round cake pans. Bake 25 to 30 minutes. Let cool 10 minutes. Remove from pans; cool completely on wire racks. Fill and frost with Chocolaty Cream Frosting (below) or your favorite frosting. Refrigerate cake until ready to serve.

CHOCOLATY CREAM FROSTING: In a large bowl, combine 1 cup confectioners' sugar, butter, Nestlé Choco-bake Unsweetened Baking Chocolate Flavor, vanilla extract and salt; beat until creamy. Beat in egg. Blend in remaining confectioners' sugar alternately with milk. Continue beating at medium speed until thick enough to spread (about 2 minutes). Fills and frosts two 8- or 9-inch cake layers.

Makes two 8- or 9-inch cake layers and 3 cups frosting

*Chocolate-Coconut Doughnuts*
*Butterscotch Banana Bread*
*Granola Coffee Ring*

# *Chocolate-Coconut Doughnuts*

## DOUGHNUTS

- **4** cups all-purpose flour
- **4** measuring teaspoons baking powder
- **3/4** measuring teaspoon salt
- **1/4** measuring teaspoon baking soda
- **2** eggs
- **1 1/4** cups sugar
- **2** envelopes (2 ounces) Nestlé Choco-bake Unsweetened Baking Chocolate Flavor
- **1/4** cup vegetable oil
- **1** measuring teaspoon coconut extract
- **3/4** cup buttermilk
  Vegetable oil

## CHOCOLATE FROSTING

- **1** envelope (1 ounce) Nestlé Choco-bake Unsweetened Baking Chocolate Flavor
- **1** cup sifted confectioners' sugar
- **2** measuring tablespoons butter, melted
- **2** measuring tablespoons boiling water
- **1/4** measuring teaspoon vanilla extract
  Toasted coconut (optional)

DOUGHNUTS: In a small bowl, combine flour, baking powder, salt and baking soda; set aside. In a large bowl, combine eggs and sugar; beat until thick and lemon colored, about 5 minutes. Stir in Choco-bake Unsweetened Baking Chocolate Flavor, oil and coconut extract. Add flour mixture alternately with buttermilk. Beat just until flour is combined. Divide dough in half; wrap each half separately with waxed paper. Chill in refrigerator about 2 hours. On a lightly floured board or pastry cloth, roll out half the dough to 1/2-inch thickness. Cut with a 3-inch doughnut cutter. Repeat with remaining chilled dough. In a deep fryer or electric skillet set at 375° F, fry doughnuts in hot oil until browned (about 1 1/2 minutes on each side). Drain on paper towels; cool. Spread tops of doughnuts with Chocolate Frosting (below). Garnish with toasted coconut, if desired.

CHOCOLATE FROSTING: In a small bowl, combine Choco-bake Unsweetened Chocolate Flavor, confectioners' sugar, butter, boiling water and vanilla extract; beat until smooth.

Makes 16 doughnuts and 1/2 cup frosting

# Chocolate Surprise Coffeecake

## CAKE

- 2 packages active dry yeast
- ¼ cup warm water
- ½ cup milk
- 1 cup butter or margarine, softened
- 1 measuring tablespoon vegetable oil
- ¼ cup sugar
- ¼ measuring teaspoon salt
- 3 cups all-purpose flour, divided
- 3 egg yolks
- 1 measuring tablespoon butter, melted

## FILLING

- 3 cups chopped walnuts
- 1 measuring teaspoon cinnamon
- 3 measuring tablespoons honey
- ½ cup milk
- ½ cup sugar
- 1 measuring teaspoon vanilla extract
- 3 egg whites
- 1 cup sugar
- 1 6-ounce package (1 cup) Nestlé Toll House Semi-Sweet Chocolate Morsels

CAKE: In a small bowl, dissolve yeast in warm water; set aside. In medium saucepan, heat milk until scalded. Add butter or margarine and vegetable oil. Cool to lukewarm. Add sugar, salt and dissolved yeast. In a large bowl, combine 2 cups flour and milk mixture; beat in egg yolks. Beat well until dough is smooth. Stir in remaining cup of flour by hand. Turn out onto floured board. Knead about 10 minutes until dough is smooth and elastic. Place in greased bowl; turn, cover and refrigerate overnight.

Preheat oven to 350°F. Divide dough in half and prepare filling (below). Roll half of dough into 20-inch x 12-inch rectangle on a well-floured board. Top with half of filling mixture, leaving 1-inch border on edge. Sprinkle with ½ cup Nestlé Toll House Semi-Sweet Chocolate Morsels. Roll up like jelly roll, starting with 20-inch side. Seal seam. Place in greased Bundt® pan; ends will overlap slightly. Repeat with remaining dough. Place on top of first dough in Bundt® pan, overlapping edges on side of pan opposite first roll. Brush with melted butter. Let rise 30 minutes, or until dough almost reaches top of pan. Bake 60 minutes. Cool 15 minutes. Remove from pan. Serve warm or cold.

FILLING: In a large saucepan, combine walnuts, cinnamon, honey, milk and ½ cup sugar. Cook over moderate heat until sugar dissolves and mixture boils. Remove from heat; cool completely. Add vanilla extract; mix well. In a small bowl, beat egg whites until frothy. Gradually add 1 cup sugar, beating until stiff peaks form. Fold egg whites into walnut mixture. Fills and frosts 2 9-inch cake layers.

Makes one 10-inch Bundt® cake

# *Granola Coffee Ring*

## CAKE

| | |
|---|---|
| 1 | cup granola |
| ¾ | cup sour cream |
| 1 | cup all-purpose flour |
| ¾ | measuring teaspoon baking soda |
| ¾ | measuring teaspoon baking powder |
| ½ | measuring teaspoon salt |
| ½ | measuring teaspoon mace |
| ½ | cup butter, softened |
| ½ | cup sugar |
| 3 | eggs |

## FILLING

| | |
|---|---|
| ½ | cup firmly packed brown sugar |
| ½ | cup chopped nuts |
| 2 | measuring tablespoons sour cream |
| ½ | measuring teaspoon cinnamon |
| 1 | 6-ounce package (1 cup) Nestlé Butterscotch Flavored Morsels |

CAKE: In a large bowl, combine granola and sour cream; let stand 15 minutes to soften cereal. Preheat oven to 350°F. In a small bowl, combine flour, baking soda, baking powder, salt and mace; set aside. Beat butter, sugar and eggs into granola-sour cream mixture. Stir in flour mixture; set aside.

FILLING: In a small bowl, mix brown sugar, nuts, sour cream and cinnamon. Spread half the granola batter into greased and floured 10-inch tube pan; dot with half the filling and sprinkle with Nestlé Butterscotch Flavored Morsels. Cover with remaining batter; top with remaining filling. Bake 50 minutes. Loosen edges. Cool cake completely; remove from pan.

Makes one 10-inch coffee cake

# Pies

Grandma's pies were good and she was proud of them. She was continuing a tradition that began with the Pilgrims. Their pies were simple, hearty fare; Grandma's, too, were delicious concoctions using the fresh fruits of the season.

Today's pies are richer — gossamer chocolate custards topped with clouds of freshly whipped cream or foamy meringue. And so the line continues, with new things building on the old. It's hard to fault a pie with its miracle of lightness and intensity of flavor, the crunchy darkness of a nut-filled chocolate shell contrasting with a froth of taste and color.

Try this collection of ethereal pies created especially for you. They're as pretty to look at as they are delicious to eat.

# Heavenly Cream Cheese Pie

**CHOCOLATE NUT CRUST**

- 1   6-ounce package (1 cup) Nestlé Toll House Semi-Sweet Chocolate Morsels
- 1   measuring tablespoon vegetable shortening
- 1½   cups finely chopped nuts

**FILLING**

- 1   6-ounce package (1 cup) Nestlé Toll House Semi-Sweet Chocolate Morsels
- 1   8-ounce package cream cheese, softened
- ¾   cup sugar, divided
- ⅛   measuring teaspoon salt
- 2   eggs, separated
- 1   cup heavy cream
- 3   measuring tablespoons brandy
-   Whipped cream for garnish (optional)

CHOCOLATE NUT CRUST: Line a 9-inch pie pan with foil. Over hot (not boiling) water, melt Nestlé Toll House Semi-Sweet Chocolate Morsels and shortening; stir in nuts. Spread evenly on bottom and side (not over rim) of prepared pie pan. Chill in refrigerator until firm (about 1 hour). Lift out of pan; peel off foil. Replace crust in pan; chill until ready to fill.

FILLING: Melt Nestlé Toll House Semi-Sweet Chocolate Morsels over hot (not boiling) water; cool 10 minutes. In a large bowl, combine cream cheese, ½ cup sugar and the salt; beat until creamy. Beat in egg yolks, one at a time. Stir in cooled chocolate; set aside. In a small bowl, beat egg whites until foamy. Gradually add ¼ cup sugar and beat until stiff, glossy peaks form. Set aside. In a small bowl, beat heavy cream and brandy until stiff peaks form. Fold whipped cream and beaten egg whites into chocolate mixture. Pour into Chocolate Nut Crust. Chill in refrigerator or until firm (about 3 hours). Garnish with whipped cream, if desired.

Makes one 9-inch pie

# Grasshopper Tarts

1   6-ounce package (1 cup) Nestlé Toll House Semi-Sweet
    Chocolate Morsels
1   measuring tablespoon vegetable shortening
1½  cups finely chopped nuts
    Grasshopper Pie filling or flavor variation (page 84)

Line 10 tart or muffin cups with foil. Over hot (not boiling) water, melt Nestlé Toll House Semi-Sweet Chocolate Morsels and shortening. Add chopped nuts; mix well. Spoon 2 measuring tablespoons mixture into prepared cups; spread evenly on bottom and up sides, using a spatula or spoon. Chill in refrigerator until firm (about 1 hour). Peel foil liners from chocolate cups. Place on serving plate. Using a pastry bag fitted with a decorative tip, pipe Grasshopper Pie filling (or flavor variation) into each chocolate cup. Chill until firm (about 1 hour).

Makes 10 tarts

# Chocolate Cream Pie

1    11½-ounce package (2 cups) Nestlé Milk Chocolate
     Morsels, divided
1    measuring tablespoon vegetable shortening
1½   cups finely chopped nuts
1    3¾-ounce package vanilla *instant* pudding and pie filling
1    cup sour cream
1    cup milk
1    cup heavy cream, sweetened and whipped

CHOCOLATE SHELL: Line a 9-inch pie pan with foil. Over hot (not boiling) water, melt 1 cup Nestlé Milk Chocolate Morsels and the shortening; stir in nuts. Spread evenly on bottom and side (not over rim) of prepared pie pan. Chill until firm (about 1 hour). Lift shell out of pan; peel off foil. Replace shell in pan; chill.

FILLING: Melt 1 cup Nestlé Milk Chocolate Morsels over hot (not boiling) water. Remove from heat; set aside. In a small bowl, combine instant pudding powder, sour cream and milk; mix well. Beat in melted chocolate. Pour into prepared Chocolate Shell. Chill in refrigerator about 2 hours. Before serving, garnish top with sweetened whipped cream.

Makes one 9-inch pie

# Grasshopper Pie

## CHOCO-NUT CRUST

1    **6-ounce package (1 cup) Nestlé Toll House Semi-Sweet Chocolate Morsels**
1    **measuring tablespoon vegetable shortening**
1½    **cups finely chopped nuts**

## FILLING

½    **pound marshmallows (about 40 large)**
⅓    **cup milk**
¼    **measuring teaspoon salt**
3    **measuring tablespoons green crème de menthe**
3    **measuring tablespoons white crème de cacao**
1½    **cups heavy cream, whipped**

CHOCO-NUT CRUST: Line a 9-inch pie pan with foil. Over hot (not boiling) water, melt Nestlé Toll House Semi-Sweet Chocolate Morsels and shortening. Add chopped nuts; mix well. Spread evenly on bottom and side (not over rim) of prepared pie pan. Chill in refrigerator until firm (about 1 hour). Lift shell out of pan; peel off foil. Replace shell in pan or place on serving plate; chill in refrigerator.

FILLING: Over hot (not boiling) water, combine marshmallows, milk and salt; heat until marshmallows melt. Remove from heat. Add liqueurs; stir until blended. Chill in refrigerator, stirring occasionally until slightly thickened (about 30 to 45 minutes). Gently fold in whipped cream. Pour half the filling into prepared Choco-Nut Crust; spoon on remaining filling, forming a design. Garnish with Chocolate Curls (page 113), if desired. Chill until firm (about 1 hour).

Makes one 9-inch pie

*FLAVOR VARIATIONS: Substitute the following for the crème de menthe and crème de cacao. Garnish as indicated.*

**Substitute:** *3 measuring tablespoons almond liqueur.* **Garnish:** *Toasted slivered almonds.*

**Substitute:** *¼ cup coffee liqueur and ¼ cup vodka.* **Garnish:** *Chopped Nestlé Toll House Semi-Sweet Chocolate Morsels.*

**Substitute:** *3 measuring tablespoons orange liqueur; 1 measuring teaspoon grated orange rind.* **Garnish:** *Orange rind slivers.*

*Grasshopper Pie; Grasshopper Tarts filled with
orange liqueur and coffee liqueur flavor variations*

# *Pumpkin Chiffon Pie*

## CHOCO-WALNUT CRUST

1   6-ounce package (1 cup) Nestlé Toll House Semi-Sweet Chocolate Morsels

2   measuring tablespoons vegetable shortening

1   cup finely chopped walnuts

## PUMPKIN CHIFFON FILLING

3/4   cup sugar, divided

1   envelope (1 measuring tablespoon) unflavored gelatin

1/2   measuring teaspoon salt

1/2   measuring teaspoon cinnamon

1/4   measuring teaspoon nutmeg

3/4   cup milk

2   eggs, separated

1   cup canned pumpkin

1   measuring teaspoon vanilla extract

1/2   cup heavy cream, whipped

CHOCO-WALNUT CRUST: Line a 9-inch pie pan with foil. Over hot (not boiling) water, melt Nestlé Toll House Semi-Sweet Chocolate Morsels and shortening; stir in walnuts. Spread evenly on bottom and side (not over rim) of prepared pie pan. Chill in refrigerator until firm (about 1 hour). Lift out of pan; peel off foil. Replace shell in pan; chill in refrigerator until ready to fill.

PUMPKIN CHIFFON FILLING: In a large saucepan, combine 1/2 cup sugar, the gelatin, salt, cinnamon and nutmeg. Stir in milk, egg yolks and pumpkin. Cook over medium heat until mixture boils and gelatin dissolves. Remove from heat; add vanilla extract. Transfer mixture to a small bowl. Set bowl over an ice bath; chill until mixture mounds from a spoon (about 30 minutes). In a small bowl, beat egg whites until soft peaks form. Gradually add remaining 1/4 cup sugar and beat until stiff peaks form. Fold into pumpkin mixture alternately with whipped cream. Pour into prepared Choco-Walnut Crust. Chill until firm (about 1 hour).

Makes one 9-inch pie

*From top: Pumpkin Chiffon Pie,*
*Chocolate-Coconut Mousse Pie*

# Chocolate-Coconut Mousse Pie

**COCONUT CRUST**

  ¼    **cup butter**

  2    **3⅓-ounce cans (2⅔ cups) shredded coconut**

**CHOCOLATE MOUSSE FILLING**

  1    **11½-ounce package (2 cups) Nestlé Milk Chocolate Morsels**

  ¼    **pound (16 large) marshmallows**

  ½    **cup milk**

  ⅛    **measuring teaspoon salt**

  1    **cup heavy cream**

COCONUT CRUST: Melt butter in a large skillet. Add coconut; stir occasionally until lightly toasted. Press evenly on bottom and side (not over rim) of buttered 9-inch pie pan. Chill in refrigerator 30 minutes.

CHOCOLATE MOUSSE FILLING: Over hot (not boiling) water, combine Nestlé Milk Chocolate Morsels, marshmallows, milk and salt; heat until morsels and marshmallows melt and mixture is smooth. Cool mixture thoroughly in refrigerator (1 to 1½ hours).

In a small bowl, beat heavy cream until stiff peaks form. Fold into cooled chocolate mixture. Pour into prepared Coconut Crust. Chill in refrigerator at least 2 hours before serving.

Makes one 9-inch pie

# Black Bottom Pie

1  cup sugar, divided
1/4  cup cornstarch
2  cups milk, scalded
3  eggs, separated
1  6-ounce package (1 cup) Nestlé Toll House Semi-Sweet
   Chocolate Morsels
2 1/2 measuring tablespoons vanilla extract, divided
1  9-inch baked pie shell
1/4  cup cold water
1  envelope (1 measuring tablespoon) unflavored gelatin
1/4  measuring teaspoon cream of tartar
1/2  cup heavy cream, whipped
   Chocolate shavings (optional)

CHOCOLATE LAYER: In a large saucepan, combine 1/2 cup sugar and the cornstarch; mix well. Gradually stir in scalded milk. Add some of the hot milk mixture to the egg yolks; mix well. Return to remaining milk mixture. Cook over moderate heat, stirring constantly, until mixture thickens (about 5 minutes). Remove 1 cup hot milk mixture to a small bowl; add Nestlé Toll House Semi-Sweet Chocolate Morsels and 1 1/2 measuring teaspoons vanilla extract. Stir until morsels melt and mixture is smooth. Pour into prepared pie shell; set aside.

VANILLA LAYER: In a large bowl, combine cold water, gelatin and 2 measuring tablespoons vanilla extract; let stand 5 minutes. Add remaining hot milk mixture from saucepan; stir until gelatin dissolves. Cool 15 minutes at room temperature. Cover surface with plastic wrap or waxed paper. In a small bowl, combine egg whites and cream of tartar; beat until foamy. Gradually add 1/2 cup sugar; beat until stiff peaks form. Fold into cooled gelatin mixture along with whipped cream. Pour over chocolate layer. Chill in refrigerator until set (about 2 hours). Garnish top of pie with chocolate shavings, if desired.

Makes one 9-inch pie

# Chocolate-Almond Pie

1    6-ounce package (1 cup) Nestlé Toll House Semi-Sweet
      Chocolate Morsels
1    cup light corn syrup
3    eggs
1/3    cup sugar
1/4    cup butter, melted
1/2    measuring teaspoon salt
1    cup coarsely chopped almonds, toasted
1    9-inch unbaked pie shell
      Whipped cream and whole almonds for garnish (optional)

Preheat oven to 375°F. Melt Nestlé Toll House Semi-Sweet Chocolate Morsels over hot (not boiling) water; remove from heat and cool at room temperature 5 minutes. In a large bowl, combine corn syrup, eggs, sugar, butter and salt; beat well. Gradually blend in melted chocolate; beat until smooth. Stir in chopped almonds. Pour into unbaked pie shell. Bake 45 to 50 minutes. Cool. Garnish with dollops of whipped cream and whole almonds, if desired.

Makes one 9-inch pie

# Chocolate Velvet Pie

4    cups miniature marshmallows
1/3    cup milk
2    envelopes (2 ounces) Nestlé Choco-bake Unsweetened Baking
      Chocolate Flavor
2    measuring teaspoons grated orange rind
1    cup heavy cream, whipped
1    9-inch baked pie shell
      Whipped cream (optional)
      Chocolate Curls (optional)

In medium saucepan, combine marshmallows and milk. Cook stirring constantly, until marshmallows are melted. Remove from heat. Stir in Nestlé Choco-bake Unsweetened Baking Chocolate Flavor and orange rind; mix well. Transfer to a small bowl; chill until slightly thickened (about 30 minutes). Stir until well blended. Fold in whipped cream. Pour into baked pie shell. Chill until firm (about 1 hour). Garnish with whipped cream and Chocolate Curls (page 149), if desired.

Makes one 9-inch pie

*Chocolate Velvet Pie*

# Chilled and Frozen Desserts

*It used to be, half a century or more ago, the children who prepared dessert for summer Sunday dinners. Squatting in the sun-dappled shade, they smashed hunks of ice in burlap bags with wooden mallets. Once the precious cylinder containing the cream was inserted in the wooden bucket, they surrounded it with crushed ice and rock salt and, amidst amiable bickering, took turns cranking until the handle would move no more. It was hot work, but at the end there was the prize—the dasher to lick, with each helper getting a share. And the family was provided with a lavish dessert, cool perfection to wind up a summer meal.*

*The air of timeless leisure created by those luscious ice-cream desserts can be recaptured in the recipes in this chapter. They will get you down to the chocolate heart of matters with an array as dazzling to the eye as tempting to the taste. Cooling in the summer and soothing after elaborate dinners, they will shine as the crown jewels of your well-set table.*

# Chocolate-Mint Soufflé

1   6-ounce package (1 cup) Nestlé Toll House Semi-Sweet
    Chocolate Morsels
1   envelope (1 measuring tablespoon) unflavored gelatin
1   cup sugar, divided
6   eggs, separated
½   cup milk
¼   cup water
1   measuring teaspoon peppermint extract
    Green food coloring
¼   measuring teaspoon salt
1   cup heavy cream, whipped

Prepare a 2-inch foil collar for a 1¼- to 1½-quart soufflé dish.
Lightly oil collar and fasten to dish; set aside. In blender container,
process Nestlé Toll House Semi-Sweet Chocolate Morsels at high
speed about 15 seconds or until reduced to fine particles; set
aside, reserving 1 measuring tablespoon for garnish. In a large
saucepan, combine gelatin and ½ cup sugar; set aside. In a small
bowl, beat egg yolks with milk and water; blend into gelatin mixture. Cook over moderate heat, stirring constantly with a wire
whisk, until gelatin is completely dissolved, and mixture thickens
slightly and coats a spoon (about 8 to 10 minutes). Stir in peppermint extract and food coloring. Cool at room temperature 15 to
20 minutes, stirring occasionally (mixture will be lukewarm).

In a large bowl, beat egg whites and salt until soft peaks form.
Gradually beat in remaining ½ cup sugar until stiff peaks form; set
aside. Gently fold peppermint-egg yolk mixture, whipped cream
and ground chocolate into egg whites. Turn into prepared soufflé
dish. Sprinkle top with reserved morsels. Chill in refrigerator until
firm (about 4 to 5 hours). Remove collar before serving.

Makes 6 to 8 servings

*MOCHA SOUFFLÉ: Omit peppermint extract and green food
coloring. Add 2 measuring tablespoons instant coffee to combined gelatin and sugar.*

*Chocolate-Mint Soufflé*

# Chocolate-Orange Puffs

ORANGE PUFFS
- ½ cup water
- ¼ cup butter
- 1 measuring tablespoon grated orange rind
  Dash salt
- ½ cup all-purpose flour
- 2 eggs
  Confectioners' sugar

CHOCOLATE FILLING
- 1 6-ounce package (1 cup) Nestlé Toll House Semi-Sweet Chocolate Morsels
- 3 measuring tablespoons orange juice
- ⅔ cup heavy cream
- 3 measuring tablespoons confectioners' sugar
  Dash salt

ORANGE PUFFS: Preheat oven to 450°F. In a small saucepan, combine water, butter, orange rind and salt; heat until mixture boils. Remove from heat. Add flour; blend until mixture holds together. Add eggs, one at a time, beating well after each addition. Drop dough by level measuring tablespoonfuls onto ungreased cookie sheets. Bake 10 minutes. Reduce heat to 350°F; bake 10 minutes longer. Remove from oven. While still hot, cut a thin slice from top of each puff. Cool completely. Spoon about 1 rounded measuring tablespoonful Chocolate Filling (below) into each puff. Replace top. Dust top with confectioners' sugar. Chill in refrigerator about 1 hour or until ready to serve.

CHOCOLATE FILLING: Over hot (not boiling) water, combine Nestlé Toll House Semi-Sweet Chocolate Morsels and orange juice; stir until morsels melt and mixture is smooth. Transfer to a large bowl; cool 10 minutes. In a small bowl, combine heavy cream, confectioners' sugar and salt; beat until stiff peaks form. Gently fold into cooled chocolate mixture.

Makes 16 puffs

# Chocolate Cappuccino Mousse Pie

## CHOCOLATE CRUMB CRUST

| | |
|---|---|
| 1 | 8½-ounce package chocolate wafers |
| 4 | measuring tablespoons butter, melted |
| ½ | measuring teaspoon cinnamon |
| ¼ | measuring teaspoon nutmeg |

## CHOCOLATE CAPPUCCINO FILLING

| | |
|---|---|
| 1 | 12-ounce package (2 cups) Nestlé Toll House Semi-Sweet Chocolate Morsels |
| 2 | measuring tablespoons butter |
| 4 | eggs, separated |
| 3 | measuring tablespoons orange liqueur |
| 2 | cups heavy cream |
| 1½ | measuring tablespoons instant coffee |
| ⅓ | cup sifted confectioners' sugar |
| | Cinnamon (optional) |
| | Nutmeg (optional) |
| | Maraschino cherry slices (optional) |

CHOCOLATE CRUMB CRUST: Preheat oven to 325°F. In blender container, grind chocolate wafers until crumbs are very fine. Transfer to a small bowl. Add butter, cinnamon and nutmeg; mix well. Pat into bottom and up sides of a 10-inch pie plate. Bake 10 minutes. Remove from oven and cool completely.

CHOCOLATE CAPPUCCINO FILLING: In a medium heavy gauge saucepan, combine Nestlé Toll House Semi-Sweet Chocolate Morsels, butter and egg yolks. Cook over very low heat stirring occasionally until mixture is melted and smooth. Remove from heat; transfer to a large bowl. In a small bowl, beat egg whites until stiff peaks form. Mix about ¼ cup beaten egg whites into chocolate mixture. Fold in remaining egg whites and orange liqueur. In a small bowl, combine heavy cream, instant coffee and confectioners' sugar. Beat until stiff. Reserve 1 cup whipped cream for garnish. Fold remaining whipped cream into chocolate mixture. Pour into prepared Chocolate Crumb Crust. Chill in refrigerator for 15 minutes until filling is slightly set. Garnish with reserved whipped cream. Lightly sprinkle whipped cream with cinnamon and nutmeg. Top with maraschino cherry slices, if desired. Freeze at least 8 hours or overnight. Remove from freezer to refrigerator 30 minutes before serving. Cut into small wedges.

Makes one 10-inch pie

# Blender Mousse

1    12-ounce package (2 cups) Nestlé Toll House Semi-Sweet
      Chocolate Morsels
½    cup sugar
3    eggs
1    cup hot milk
2    to 4 measuring tablespoons brandy, rum, or almond or
      orange liqueurs
      Whipped cream (optional)

In blender container, combine Nestlé Toll House Semi-Sweet
Chocolate Morsels, sugar and eggs. Add hot milk and liquor;
blend at medium speed until mixture is smooth. Pour into pots de
crème or demitasse cups and chill in refrigerator 1 hour. Garnish
with whipped cream, if desired. *Keep in refrigerator* until ready
to serve.

Makes 8 4-ounce servings

*MOCHA MOUSSE: Add 3 measuring tablespoons instant coffee
to blender along with eggs.*

# Chocolate Mousse

1    6-ounce package (1 cup) Nestlé Toll House Semi-Sweet
      Chocolate Morsels
3    eggs, separated
¼    cup water
⅛    teaspoon salt
⅓    cup firmly packed brown sugar

Melt Nestlé Toll House Semi-Sweet Chocolate Morsels over hot
(not boiling) water; remove from heat. Add egg yolks, one at a
time, beating well after each addition. Add water; beat until
smooth. In a small bowl, combine egg whites and salt; beat until
soft peaks form. Gradually beat in brown sugar and continue
beating until stiff, glossy peaks form. Gently fold in chocolate mixture. Chill in refrigerator several hours or until ready to serve.

Makes 4 to 6 servings

*Note:* Because it contains raw eggs, be sure to keep mousse refrigerated.

*Blender Mousse, Butterscotch Thins*

# Frozen Mocha Charlotte

2 measuring teaspoons butter, softened
2 measuring tablespoons sugar
2 3-ounce packages ladyfingers
1/4 cup light rum
1 12-ounce package (2 cups) Nestlé Toll House Semi-Sweet Chocolate Morsels
3 measuring tablespoons instant coffee
1/2 cup boiling water
6 eggs, separated
1/2 cup sugar
1/2 measuring teaspoon vanilla extract
1/4 measuring teaspoon coconut extract
2 cups heavy cream, whipped
1/4 cup ground nuts

Butter a 9-inch round springform pan with 2 teaspoons butter. Sprinkle with 2 tablespoons sugar; set aside. Split ladyfingers (do not separate); brush inside surface with rum. Line side of prepared springform pan with ladyfingers, rounded sides against pan. Separate remaining ladyfingers and line bottom of pan to fit. Melt Nestlé Toll House Semi-Sweet Chocolate Morsels over hot (not boiling) water; set aside. In a small measuring cup, combine instant coffee and boiling water; stir until dissolved. Set aside. In a large bowl, beat egg yolks until foamy. Gradually beat in 1/2 cup sugar at high speed until thick and lemon colored (about 4 minutes). Beat in melted chocolate, coffee mixture, and vanilla and coconut extracts; set aside. In a large bowl, beat egg whites until stiff. Fold egg whites and 3 cups of the whipped cream into chocolate mixture. Pour into ladyfinger-lined pan. Freeze until firm (about 2 hours). Pipe rosettes with remaining whipped cream and sprinkle with ground nuts. Allow charlotte to thaw one hour at room temperature before serving. Remove springform ring before serving. Refrigerate leftover charlotte.

Makes 10 to 12 servings

# Chocolate Dessert Waffles

1 1/2 cups milk
1 cup sugar
3 envelopes (3 ounces) Nestlé Choco-bake
1 egg
2 measuring tablespoons vegetable oil
3/4 measuring teaspoon vanilla extract
3/4 measuring teaspoon cinnamon
2 cups buttermilk pancake mix
Ice cream
Chocolate sauce

In blender container or a large bowl, combine milk, sugar, Nestlé Choco-bake, egg, oil, vanilla extract and cinnamon; process at medium speed about 10 seconds or beat well. Add pancake mix; blend until smooth (about 1 minute), scraping sides of container if necessary. To bake waffles, follow manufacturer's instructions on waffle iron. Serve with ice cream and chocolate sauce.

Makes 20 3x5-inch waffles

# *Ruby Pears with Chocolate Cream*

**RUBY PEARS**

| | |
|---|---|
| 2 | 29-ounce cans pear halves, drained |
| 2 | cups ginger ale |
| | Juice of 1 orange |
| | Juice of ½ lime |
| 2 | measuring tablespoons butter or margarine, melted |
| 1 | cinnamon stick |
| 3 | whole cloves |
| 1½ | cups red currant jelly |

**CHOCOLATE CREAM**

| | |
|---|---|
| 1 | 6-ounce package (1 cup) Nestlé Toll House Semi-Sweet Chocolate Morsels |
| 2 | measuring tablespoons honey |
| 1½ | measuring tablespoons light rum |
| 1½ | cups heavy cream, whipped |

PEARS: Preheat oven to 350°F. Arrange pears, cut side up, in 13x9x2-inch baking pan. In a small bowl, combine ginger ale, orange juice, lime juice, butter or margarine, cinnamon stick and cloves; mix well. Pour over pears. Cover pan with aluminum foil; refrigerate overnight. Remove from refrigerator; allow to sit at room temperature 30 minutes. Cover with aluminum foil. Bake 30 minutes. Remove from oven. Drain pears, reserving 5 measuring tablespoons liquid. Place pears into serving dishes; set aside. In a small saucepan, melt red currant jelly over low heat. Add 3 measuring tablespoons reserved liquid; mix well. Pour equally over pears. Serve with Chocolate Cream (below).

CHOCOLATE CREAM: Over hot (not boiling) water, combine Nestlé Toll House Semi-Sweet Chocolate Morsels, honey and 2 measuring tablespoons reserved liquid; stir until morsels melt and mixture is smooth. Remove from heat; transfer to a small bowl. Add rum. Fold in whipped cream.

Makes 8 to 10 servings and about 3 cups Chocolate Cream

*Chocolate Bavarian*

# Chocolate Bavarian

2   envelopes (2 measuring tablespoons) unflavored gelatin
1   cup sugar, divided
1/4   measuring teaspoon salt
4   eggs, separated
2   cups milk
1   12-ounce package (2 cups) Nestlé Toll House
     Semi-Sweet Chocolate Morsels
2   measuring teaspoons vanilla extract
2   cups heavy cream, whipped
    Whipped Cream for garnish (optional)
    Chocolate Curls, page 113 (optional)

In a large saucepan, combine gelatin, 1/2 cup sugar and the salt. In a small bowl, beat egg yolks and milk; stir into gelatin mixture. Add Nestlé Toll House Semi-Sweet Chocolate Morsels and cook over medium heat, stirring constantly, until morsels are melted and gelatin is dissolved (about 8 minutes). Remove from heat and stir in vanilla extract. Chill, stirring occasionally, until mixture mounds when dropped from a spoon. In a small bowl, beat egg whites until stiff but not dry. Gradually add remaining 1/2 cup sugar, beating until very stiff. Fold in chilled chocolate mixture alternately with whipped cream. Turn into 8-cup decorative mold. Chill in refrigerator until firm. Unmold onto a serving platter. Garnish with whipped cream and/or Chocolate Curls, if desired.

Makes 12 servings

# Blender Chocolate Ice Cream

1/2   cup sugar
1/2   cup water
1   6-ounce package (1 cup) Nestlé Toll House Semi-Sweet
    Chocolate Morsels
2   eggs
2   measuring teaspoons vanilla extract
1/2   measuring teaspoon salt
1 1/2   cups heavy cream, whipped

In a small saucepan, combine sugar and water. Bring to a boil over moderate heat; boil 3 minutes, then remove from heat. In blender container, combine Nestlé Toll House Semi-Sweet Chocolate Morsels and hot sugar syrup; process at high speed about 6 seconds. Add eggs, vanilla extract and salt; blend for about 1 minute. Pour over whipped cream and mix well. Pour into 9x5x3-inch loaf pan. Freeze until firm.

Makes 1 quart ice cream

# Special Occasion Desserts

Traditions enrich life, stitching texture into its fabric. Whether it be the annual gathering of friends and family to celebrate the holidays, the remembrance of a birthday or anniversary or the celebration of some other occasion, your family expresses itself in its own special ways.

Food forms the background of these celebrations. The rite of preparing the Christmas fruitcakes takes on a significance of its own. The special huge mixing bowl used but once a year, the nuts and candied fruits to chop, the rich cakes to wrap as gifts and the large cake for the family celebration—all become symbols of your love and concern.

Because we realize the importance of this symbolism, we created some special desserts tailored for special occasions. We know you'll soon find them part of your family tradition, a tradition that will be carried on.

# Chocolate Soufflé

Butter
2  measuring tablespoons graham cracker crumbs
3  measuring tablespoons butter
3  measuring tablespoons all-purpose flour
1  cup milk
1  6-ounce package (1 cup) Nestlé Toll House Semi-Sweet
   Chocolate Morsels
4  eggs, separated
¼  cup rum
1  measuring teaspoon vanilla extract
   Vanilla ice cream or sweetened whipped cream

Butter bottom and sides of a 6-cup soufflé dish; coat with graham cracker crumbs. In a small saucepan, melt 3 measuring tablespoons butter over medium heat. Blend in flour. Gradually stir in milk. Cook, stirring constantly, until mixture thickens. Stir in Nestlé Toll House Semi-Sweet Chocolate Morsels. Transfer chocolate mixture to a large bowl; cool 10 minutes. Beat in egg yolks, rum and vanilla extract; set aside.

Preheat oven to 350°F. In a small bowl, beat egg whites until stiff (not dry) peaks form. Stir ½ cup beaten egg whites into chocolate mixture. Gently fold remaining egg whites into chocolate mixture. Pour into prepared dish. For a top-hat soufflé, run knife through batter in a circle 1 inch from edge of dish, to a depth of 1 inch. Bake 40 minutes. Serve immediately with vanilla ice cream or sweetened whipped cream.

Makes 6 to 8 servings

# Meringue Mushrooms

2  egg whites, at room temperature
⅛  measuring teaspoon salt
⅛  measuring teaspoon cream of tartar
¼  measuring teaspoon vanilla extract
½  cup sugar
   Nestlé Quik Chocolate Flavor
1  6-ounce package (1 cup) Nestlé Toll House Semi-Sweet
   Chocolate Morsels, melted (optional)

Preheat oven to 250°F. In a small bowl, beat egg whites until foamy. Add salt, cream of tartar and vanilla extract; beat until soft peaks form. Gradually add sugar, 2 tablespoons at a time, beating at high speed until stiff peaks form. Fill a pastry bag fitted with large writing tip with meringue. Pipe 15 mounds resembling mushroom caps (1 to 1½ inches in diameter) onto foil-lined cookie sheet. On another foil-lined cookie sheet, pipe 15 "mushroom stems" (1 to 1½ inches long). Lightly sift Quik evenly over caps and stems. Bake 25 to 35 minutes. Cool completely. To remove, peel back foil or loosen with metal spatula. Make a small hole in bottom of each cap. Insert pointed end of stem into hole. Bottoms of caps may be decorated with melted Nestlé Toll House Semi-Sweet Morsels, if desired. Store in tightly covered container.

Makes 15 to 20 assorted-size meringue mushrooms

# *Butterscotch-Nut Crêpes*

## CRÊPES

| | |
|---|---|
| 1¼ | cups milk |
| 1 | cup buttermilk pancake mix |
| 1 | egg |
| 1 | measuring tablespoon vegetable oil |
| 2 | measuring tablespoons butter, melted |

## BUTTERSCOTCH-NUT FILLING

| | |
|---|---|
| 1 | 6-ounce package (1 cup) Nestlé Butterscotch Flavored Morsels |
| 2 | measuring tablespoons corn syrup |
| 2 | measuring tablespoons butter |
| 2 | measuring teaspoons water |
| 1¼ | measuring teaspoons grated orange rind |
| ¼ | measuring teaspoon salt |
| 1 | cup finely ground nuts |

## GARNISH

Whipped cream

CRÊPES: In a small bowl, combine milk, pancake mix, egg and oil; beat until mixture is smooth. Heat an 8-inch crêpe pan or skillet; brush with butter. For each crêpe, pour about 3 measuring tablespoons batter into pan; turn and tip pan immediately to coat bottom. Cook 10 to 15 seconds until lightly browned and set on top; turn and cook other side. Remove crêpe to a heated platter. Repeat with remaining batter. Spread 1 rounded measuring tablespoonful Butterscotch-Nut Filling (below) over each crêpe. Fold into triangles or roll up jelly-roll fashion; place on a serving platter. Spoon remaining filling over crêpes and serve with whipped cream.

BUTTERSCOTCH-NUT FILLING: Over hot (not boiling) water, combine Nestlé Butterscotch Flavored Morsels, corn syrup, butter, water, orange rind and salt; stir until morsels melt and mixture is smooth. Add nuts; mix well.

Makes 8 filled crêpes

*CHOCOLATE-NUT CRÊPES: In the filling, substitute one 6-ounce package (1 cup) Nestlé Toll House Semi-Sweet Chocolate Morsels for Nestlé Butterscotch Flavored Morsels and vanilla extract for grated orange rind.*

# Party Chocolate Crêpes

## CRÊPES

- **1** 6-ounce package (1 cup) Nestlé Toll House Semi-Sweet Chocolate Morsels
- **3** measuring tablespoons butter
- **1** cup all-purpose flour
- **1** cup sifted confectioners' sugar
- **4** eggs
- **½** cup milk
- **½** cup water
- **1** measuring tablespoon vanilla extract
- **1** measuring teaspoon salt
  Melted butter
  Confectioners' sugar

## ORANGE CREAM CHEESE FILLING

- **3** 8-ounce packages cream cheese, softened
- **¾** cup sifted confectioners' sugar
- **½** cup milk
- **2** measuring tablespoons grated orange rind

CRÊPES: Over hot (not boiling) water, combine Nestlé Toll House Semi-Sweet Chocolate Morsels and butter; heat until morsels melt and mixture is smooth. Remove from heat; cool slightly. In blender container, combine cooled chocolate mixture, flour, confectioners' sugar, eggs, milk, water, vanilla extract and salt; blend at medium speed until smooth (about 2 minutes), scraping sides of container when necessary. Brush a 6- or 8-inch crêpe pan or skillet with melted butter. When butter begins to sizzle, pour about 3 measuring tablespoonfuls batter into pan; turn and tip pan immediately to coat bottom. Cook until top of crêpe begins to dry (about 20 seconds); turn and cook a few seconds. Remove from pan. Repeat with remaining batter. Spread 2 level measuring tablespoonfuls Orange Cream Cheese Filling (below) over each crêpe. Roll up jelly-roll fashion; place on a platter. Dust with confectioners' sugar.

ORANGE CREAM CHEESE FILLING: In a large bowl, combine cream cheese, confectioners' sugar, milk and grated orange rind; beat until smooth and creamy.

Makes 15 servings (30 filled crêpes)

*Butterscotch-Nut Crêpes*
*Party Chocolate Crêpes*

# Brownie Torte

1    **12-ounce package (2 cups) Nestlé Toll House Semi-Sweet Chocolate Morsels**
1    **cup butter**
1½    **cups sugar**
4    **eggs**
1½    **cups all-purpose flour**
1    **cup chopped nuts**
2    **cups heavy cream**
3    **measuring tablespoons confectioners' sugar**

Preheat oven to 375°F. Combine Nestlé Toll House Semi-Sweet Chocolate Morsels and butter over hot (not boiling) water; heat until morsels melt and mixture is smooth. Pour into a large bowl. Mix in sugar. Add eggs, one at a time, beating well after each addition. Gradually blend in flour. Stir in nuts. Pour into three greased and floured 9-inch round cake pans. Bake 15 to 20 minutes. Cool 10 minutes. Remove from pans; cool completely. In a large bowl, combine heavy cream and confectioners' sugar; beat until stiff peaks form. To assemble, spread a third of the whipped cream over each of 2 brownie layers. Decorate third layer with dollops of remaining whipped cream or pipe through pastry tube. Stack layers, placing decorated layer on top. Chill in refrigerator until ready to serve.

Makes one 9-inch torte

# Rich Hot Chocolate

1    **6-ounce package (1 cup) Nestlé Toll House Semi-Sweet Chocolate Morsels**
1    **cup water**
2½    **cups milk**
1½    **cups heavy cream**
   **Dash salt**
2    **measuring tablespoons brandy or 1 measuring tablespoon instant coffee (optional)**

Over hot (not boiling) water, combine Nestlé Toll House Semi-Sweet Chocolate Morsels and water; heat until morsels melt and mixture is smooth. In a large saucepan, combine milk, cream and salt; bring *just to a boil*. Add chocolate mixture to milk mixture; stir until heated through. Stir in brandy or coffee, if desired, for added flavor.

Makes 6 servings

# *Heavenly Butterscotch Torte*

## CAKE

| | |
|---|---|
| 1 | 6-ounce package (1 cup) Nestlé Butterscotch Flavored Morsels |
| 2 | cups all-purpose flour |
| 1 | measuring teaspoon baking soda |
| 1 | measuring teaspoon baking powder |
| 1 | measuring teaspoon mace |
| 1/2 | measuring teaspoon salt |
| 1 | cup sugar |
| 3/4 | cup vegetable oil |
| 1 | measuring teaspoon vanilla extract |
| 3 | eggs |
| 1 | cup buttermilk or sour milk* |
| 1/4 | cup orange liqueur or orange juice |

## CHOCOLATE ANGEL FROSTING

| | |
|---|---|
| 1 | 6-ounce package (1 cup) Nestlé Toll House Semi-Sweet Chocolate Morsels |
| 1/2 | cup sour cream |
| 1 | measuring teaspoon vanilla extract |
| 1/4 | measuring teaspoon salt |
| 2 1/2 | cups sifted confectioners' sugar |

CAKE: Preheat oven to 350°F. Melt Nestlé Butterscotch Flavored Morsels over hot (not boiling) water. In a small bowl, combine flour, baking soda, baking powder, mace and salt; set aside. In a large bowl combine sugar, oil, melted butterscotch and vanilla extract; beat until creamy. Add eggs, one at a time, beating well after each addition. Blend in flour mixture alternately with buttermilk. Pour batter evenly into two greased and floured 9-inch round cake pans. Bake 45 minutes. Cool 10 minutes. Remove from pans, cool completely. Using a long, thin serrated knife, slice each layer in half crosswise and sprinkle each with 1 measuring tablespoon orange liqueur of juice. Spread top of each layer (not sides) with Chocolate Angle Frosting (below).

CHOCOLATE ANGEL FROSTING: Melt Nestlé Toll House Semi-Sweet Chocolate Morsels over hot (not boiling) water. Transfer to a small bowl. Blend in sour cream, vanilla extract and salt. Gradually beat in confectioners' sugar; mix until creamy and smooth.

Makes one 9-inch torte

*To make sour milk:* Combine 1 measuring tablespoon vinegar or lemon juice and enough sweet milk to equal 1 cup. Let stand 5 minutes.

Quick Party Log, garnished with
Chocolate Curls and Meringue Mushrooms

# Quick Party Log

1    12-ounce package (2 cups) Nestlé Toll House Semi-Sweet
     Chocolate Morsels
1    cup sour cream
1    measuring teaspoon vanilla extract
¼    measuring teaspoon salt
3    cups sifted confectioners' sugar
2    11½-ounce frozen pound cakes, thawed
     Chocolate Curls and/or chocolate shavings (optional)
     Meringue Mushrooms (optional)

Melt Nestlé Toll House Semi-Sweet Chocolate Morsels over hot
(not boiling) water. Transfer to a small bowl; cool 5 minutes.
Blend in sour cream, vanilla extract and salt. Gradually add confectioners' sugar; beat until smooth. Set frosting aside.

Place pound cakes end to end to form one long cake. To form a
log-shaped cake, round off edges by running a sharp knife down
length of cake, slicing off all four corner edges (cake should resemble a cylinder). Cut cake crosswise into three layers. Fill and
frost cake with prepared frosting. Run tines of fork lengthwise
through frosting to simulate bark. Garnish with Chocolate Curls
(below), chocolate shavings and Meringue Mushrooms (page
106), if desired.

Makes 16 slices

# Chocolate Curls

1    12-ounce package (2 cups) Nestlé Toll House Semi-Sweet
     Chocolate Morsels
¼    cup vegetable shortening

Over hot (not boiling) water, combine Nestlé Toll House Semi-
Sweet Chocolate Morsels and vegetable shortening; stir until
morsels melt and mixture is smooth. Pour into foil-lined 9x5x3-
inch loaf pan. Chill until firm (about 2 hours). Remove foil from
chocolate block. Make chocolate curls using one of the following:
vegetable peeler, cheese slicer, cheese plane, lemon zester or butter curler.* Place curls on cookie sheet; chill until ready to use.

Makes 1¼ cups melted chocolate

*If chocolate appears too brittle to curl, let stand at room temperature 30
minutes before making Chocolate Curls.

# Butterscotch-Apple Crisp

**FILLING**

- **1**   measuring tablespoon lemon juice
- **8**   cups pared, cored and sliced tart cooking apples or 3 20-ounce cans sliced apples
- **1**   cup sugar
- **½**   cup all-purpose flour
- **2**   measuring teaspoons cinnamon
- **⅛**   measuring teaspoon salt

**TOPPING**

- **1**   12-ounce package (2 cups) Nestlé Butterscotch Flavored Morsels
- **½**   cup butter
- **1½**  cups all-purpose flour
- **¼**   measuring teaspoon salt
- **¼**   measuring teaspoon mace
  Heavy cream, sweetened whipped cream or vanilla ice cream (optional)

FILLING: Preheat oven to 375°F. In a large bowl, combine lemon juice and sliced apples; toss until well coated. Stir in sugar, flour, cinnamon and salt; mix well. Turn into greased 13x9x2-inch baking pan; spread evenly. Bake 20 minutes. Crumble topping (below) over top of hot apples. Return to oven; bake 25 minutes. Serve warm with heavy cream, sweetened whipped cream or vanilla ice cream, if desired.

TOPPING: Over hot (not boiling) water, combine Nestlé Butterscotch Flavored Morsels and butter, stir until morsels melt and mixture is smooth. Remove from heat. With a fork, stir in flour, salt and mace until flour is just blended and mixture forms a large crumb.

Makes 12 servings

*Rescue breakfasts from boredom and offer a sweet surprise: warm Butterscotch-Apple Crisp (make ahead, reheat in the morning) served with a splash of heavy cream. Who'll miss the toast?*

# Chocolate-Meringue Nut Torte

**MERINGUE-NUT LAYERS**

- 3 egg whites
- 1/4 measuring teaspoon salt
- 3/4 cup firmly packed brown sugar
- 2 cups ground toasted almonds

**CHOCOLATE FILLING**

- 1 7 1/2-ounce jar marshmallow cream
- 2 to 4 measuring tablespoons bourbon
- 1 6-ounce package (1 cup) Nestlé Toll House Semi-Sweet Chocolate Morsels
- 3 egg yolks
- 1 cup heavy cream, whipped

MERINGUE-NUT LAYERS: Cut four 8-inch circles of brown paper or parchment paper; place on large cookie sheet. Set aside. Preheat oven to 300°F. In a small bowl, combine egg whites and salt; beat until foamy. Gradually beat in brown sugar until stiff peaks form; fold in almonds. Spread 3/4 cup meringue-nut mixture evenly on each paper circle, leaving a border of paper 1/4 inch wide. Bake 20 to 25 minutes. Cool completely. Very carefully, so as not to break edges, remove paper from each layer. Place one layer on cake plate; spread 3/4 cup Chocolate Filling (below) over top. Repeat with 2 more layers. Place fourth layer on top and garnish with dollops of remaining Chocolate Filling or pipe through pastry tube. Refrigerate until ready to serve.

CHOCOLATE FILLING: In a small bowl, combine marshmallow cream and bourbon; set aside. Melt Nestlé Toll House Semi-Sweet Chocolate Morsels over hot (not boiling) water; set aside. In a small bowl, beat egg yolks until thick (about 5 minutes); gradually add melted chocolate, stirring rapidly and constantly. Blend chocolate mixture into marshmallow mixture, stirring until smooth. Transfer to a large bowl. Chill in refrigerator 45 minutes (or over ice bath 15 to 20 minutes) until mixture is slightly thickened. Gently fold in whipped cream.

Makes one 9-inch torte

# Easy Chocolate Fondue

1    6-ounce package (1 cup) Nestlé Toll House Semi-Sweet
     Chocolate Morsels
½   cup corn syrup
1    measuring teaspoon vanilla extract
     Dash salt
2    to 3 measuring tablespoons brandy
     Bite-size pieces fruit (apples, bananas, seedless grapes,
      fresh strawberries, maraschino cherries or mandarin
      orange segments)
     Pound cake, cut into cubes
     Ground nuts or toasted shredded coconut (optional)

Combine Nestlé Toll House Semi-Sweet Chocolate Morsels, corn syrup, vanilla extract and salt in an electric fondue pot or a large saucepan. Stir over medium heat until morsels melt and mixture is smooth. Add brandy; mix well. Serve with your favorite fruit dippers and/or pound cake cubes. After dipping in chocolate, coat with ground nuts or shredded coconut, if desired.

Makes 1 cup fondue

# Chocolate Linzer Torte

¾   cup butter, softened
1    cup sifted confectioners' sugar
3    measuring tablespoons mayonnaise
1    measuring teaspoon cinnamon
¼   measuring teaspoon ground cloves
1½  cups all-purpose flour
1    cup coarsely chopped almonds
1    6-ounce package (1 cup) Nestlé Toll House Semi-Sweet
     Chocolate Morsels
1    cup raspberry preserves

Preheat oven to 300°F. In a large bowl, combine butter and confectioners' sugar; beat until creamy. Blend in mayonnaise, cinnamon and cloves. Gradually add flour; mix well. Stir in almonds and Nestlé Toll House Semi-Sweet Chocolate Morsels. Divide dough into two balls; cover and refrigerate 30 minutes. Place one ball of dough into 9-inch pie pan. Flatten dough to fit in bottom of pan. Spread raspberry preserves on top of dough. Roll out remaining dough between 2 sheets of waxed paper. Remove waxed paper; place dough on top of pie. Crimp edges, if desired. With sharp knife, score top crust into 16 wedges. Bake 45 minutes. Remove from oven; cool completely.

Makes one 9-inch pie

*Easy Chocolate Fondue*

# Sauces, Frostings and Glazes

Sauces for ice creams and puddings, frostings for cakes...and the little ones underfoot trying to lick the bowl. What pleasant memories to have, what pleasant times to pass...talking and working in the quiet intimacy of your kitchen, sharing its warmth and gaiety with your children.

In time the little ones will be as interested in learning how to make your "just plain good" sauces and frostings as they are in helping to clean out the bowl. That is the stuff of traditions. As your mother passed these pleasures and skills to you, so will you to your own children and they to theirs.

Center: Rich Hot Chocolate, Blender Chocolate Ice
Cream. Ice cream sauces, top to bottom: Hot Creamy
Fudge Sauce, Hot Chocolate Sauce, Orange-
Butterscotch Sauce with Chocolate Dessert Waffle.

# Hot Chocolate Sauce

- ³/₄ cup sugar
- ¹/₄ cup butter
- 2 envelopes (2 ounces) Nestlé Choco-bake Unsweetened Baking Chocolate Flavor
- 2 measuring tablespoons light corn syrup
  Dash of salt
- ¹/₄ cup milk
- 2 measuring teaspoons vanilla extract

In a small saucepan, combine sugar, butter, Nestlé Choco-bake Unsweetened Baking Chocolate Flavor, corn syrup and salt; mix well. Cook over medium heat, stirring constantly, until sugar dissolves. Add milk; bring to a boil, stirring constantly. Remove from heat; stir in vanilla extract. Serve warm over ice cream or cake.

Makes 1 cup sauce.

# Orange-Butterscotch Sauce

- 1 6-ounce package (1 cup) Nestlé Butterscotch Flavored Morsels
- ¹/₄ cup evaporated milk
- ¹/₄ measuring teaspoon orange extract

Melt Nestlé Butterscotch Flavored Morsels over hot (not boiling) water. Stir in evaporated milk and orange extract. Blend mixture with a fork or wire whisk until smooth. Serve warm over ice cream or cake.

Makes ³/₄ cup sauce

# Hot Creamy Fudge Sauce

- ¹/₂ cup milk
- ¹/₄ cup butter
- ¹/₄ measuring teaspoon salt
- 1 11¹/₂-ounce package (2 cups) Nestlé Milk Chocolate Morsels
- 1 measuring teaspoon vanilla extract

Over hot (not boiling) water, combine milk, butter and salt; heat until butter melts. Add Nestlé Milk Chocolate Morsels; stir until morsels melt and mixture is smooth. Remove from heat; stir in vanilla extract. Serve warm over ice cream, cake, waffles or pancakes.

Makes 1¹/₂ cups sauce

# Chocolate Skillet Sauce

¼     **cup butter**
1     **cup coarsely chopped nuts**
1     **6-ounce package (1 cup) Nestlé Toll House Semi-Sweet Chocolate Morsels**

Melt butter in a large skillet.* Add nuts and cook until browned, stirring constantly to prevent scorching. Remove from heat. Add Nestlé Toll House Semi-Sweet Chocolate Morsels and stir until morsels melt and mixture is blended. Serve warm over ice cream.

Makes 1¼ cups sauce

*This recipe may be made in an electric skillet set at 350°F.

**BUTTERSCOTCH SKILLET SAUCE:** *Substitute one 6-ounce package (1 cup) Nestlé Butterscotch Flavored Morsels for chocolate morsels.*

**MILK CHOCOLATE SKILLET SAUCE:** *Increase butter to ½ cup and nuts to 2 cups. Substitute one 11½-ounce package (2 cups) Nestlé Milk Chocolate Morsels for semi-sweet chocolate morsels.*

Makes 2½ cups sauce

# Hot Mocha Ice Cream Sauce

1     **6-ounce package (1 cup) Nestlé Toll House Semi-Sweet Chocolate Morsels**
¾     **cup corn syrup**
¼     **cup milk**
2     **measuring tablespoons butter**
1     **measuring teaspoon instant coffee**

In a small saucepan, combine Nestlé Toll House Semi-Sweet Chocolate Morsels and corn syrup; heat over low heat until morsels melt and mixture is smooth. Add milk, butter and coffee; stir until well blended. Remove from heat; cool 5 minutes. Serve warm over ice cream or cake.

Makes 1½ cups sauce

# Cooked Chocolate Frosting

1   cup sugar
4   envelopes (4 ounces) Nestlé Choco-bake Unsweetened Baking
    Chocolate Flavor
2/3  cup heavy cream
1/4  cup water
2   measuring tablespoons corn syrup
1   egg, slightly beaten
1   measuring teaspoon vanilla extract

In a large saucepan, combine sugar. Nestlé Choco-bake Unsweetened Baking Chocolate Flavor, cream, water and corn syrup. Cook
over moderate heat, stirring constantly until sugar dissolves. Cook
without stirring 6 minutes. Remove from heat. Blend about 3 measuring tablespoons chocolate mixture into egg and return to chocolate mixture. Stir in vanilla extract. Cook, stirring constantly, over
moderate heat, about 1 minute or until thick. Cool completely before frosting cake. Fills and frosts two 8-inch layers or one 13x9x2-
inch cake.

Makes about 2 cups frosting

# Chocolate Butter Frosting

1/4  cup milk
2   measuring tablespoons butter
1/8  measuring teaspoon salt
1   6-ounce package (1 cup) Nestlé Toll House Semi-Sweet
    Chocolate Morsels
1   measuring teaspoon vanilla extract
1 1/2 cups sifted confectioners' sugar
1   to 2 measuring teaspoons milk

In a medium saucepan, combine 1/4 cup milk, butter and salt; bring
to a boil over medium heat. Remove from heat. Add Nestlé Toll
House Semi-Sweet Chocolate Morsels and vanilla extract; stir until morsels melt and mixture is smooth. Blend in confectioners'
sugar. Stir in 1 to 2 measuring teaspoons milk until mixture is of
spreading consistency. Beat well. Frosts one 13x9x2-inch cake.

Makes 1 1/3 cups frosting

*Note:* Frosting appears thin but does cling nicely to cake.

# Rich and Creamy Chocolate Frosting

- ¼ cup butter
- ½ of 12-ounce package (1 cup) Nestle Little Bits Semi-Sweet Chocolate
- ¼ measuring teaspoon salt
- 1 measuring teaspoon vanilla extract
- 2¼ cups sifted confectioners' sugar
- 4 to 5 measuring tablespoons milk

In a small saucepan, melt butter. Stir in Nestlé Little Bits Semi-Sweet Chocolate until melted. Transfer to a small bowl. Add salt and vanilla extract. At medium speed, gradually beat in confectioners' sugar with milk until mixture is of spreading consistency. Fills and frosts two 9-inch cake layers.

Makes about 1¾ cups frosting

# Creamy Butterscotch Frosting

- 1 6-ounce package (1 cup) Nestlé Butterscotch Flavored Morsels
- 1 measuring tablespoon water
- 1 8-ounce package cream cheese, softened
- ⅛ measuring teaspoon salt
- 3 cups sifted confectioners' sugar

Over hot (not boiling) water, combine Nestlé Butterscotch Flavored Morsels and water; stir until morsels melt and mixture is smooth. Remove from heat. In a small bowl, combine cream cheese and salt; beat until creamy. Blend in melted butterscotch. Gradually add confectioners' sugar. Beat until smooth. Fills and frosts two 8- or 9-inch cake layers.

Makes 2½ cups frosting

# Sour Cream Velvet Frosting

- 1 12-ounce package (2 cups) Nestlé Toll House Semi-Sweet Chocolate Morsels
- ⅔ cup sour cream
- 1 measuring teaspoon vanilla extract
- ¼ measuring teaspoon salt
- 3 cups sifted confectioners' sugar

Melt Nestlé Toll House Semi-Sweet Chocolate Morsels over hot (not boiling) water; transfer to a large bowl and cool 5 minutes. Blend in sour cream, vanilla extract and salt. Gradually beat in confectioners' sugar; beat until smooth and creamy. Fills and frosts two 8- or 9-inch cake layers.

Makes 2⅔ cups frosting

*A medley of cupcakes topped with
Rich and Creamy Chocolate Frosting
and Creamy Butterscotch Frosting*

# Rich Chocolate Cream Frosting

1　12-ounce package (2 cups) Nestlé Toll House Semi-Sweet
　　Chocolate Morsels
1　8-ounce package cream cheese, softened
1　measuring teaspoon vanilla extract
½　measuring teaspoon salt
3¼　cups sifted confectioners' sugar
2　measuring tablespoons milk

Over hot (not boiling) water, melt Nestlé Toll House Semi-Sweet
Chocolate Morsels; remove from heat. In a large bowl, combine
melted chocolate, cream cheese, vanilla extract and salt; beat well.
Beat in confectioners' sugar alternately with milk. Fills and frosts
two 8- or 9-inch cake layers.

Makes 3 cups frosting

# Creamy Mocha Frosting

1　11½-ounce package (2 cups) Nestlé Milk Chocolate Morsels
1　measuring teaspoon instant coffee
⅔　cup sour cream
1　measuring teaspoon vanilla extract
¼　measuring teaspoon salt
3　cups sifted confectioners' sugar

Over hot (not boiling) water, melt Nestlé Milk Chocolate Morsels;
remove from heat. Stir in coffee; cool 10 minutes. In a small bowl
combine melted chocolate mixture, sour cream, vanilla extract and
salt; beat well. Gradually beat in confectioners' sugar. Fills and
frosts two 8- or 9-inch cake layers.

Makes 3 cups frosting

# Index

Apple Cartwheels, 53
Apple Crisp, Butterscotch-, 114

Baking information, 7
Banana Bread, Butterscotch, 74
Banana Pops, 40
Bavarian, Chocolate, 103
Black Bottom Pie, 89
Black Forest Cherry Torte, 69
Blender Chocolate Ice Cream, 103
Blender Mousse, 98
Blueberry Clusters, 53
Bourbon Balls, 29
**Breakfast breads**
  Butterscotch Banana Bread, 74
  Chocolate-Coconut Doughnuts, 77
  Chocolate Surprise Coffeecake, 78
  Granola Coffee Ring, 79
  Toll House Crumb Cake, 17
**Brownies**
  Butterscotch, 36
  Chocolate–Peanut Butter, 61
  Cream Cheese Ripple Squares, 39
  Double Chocolate, 13
  Double Peanut Butter, 50
  Frosted Fudge, 40
  Golden Peanut Butter, 16
  Toll House Golden, 12
  Triple-Layer, 36
Brownie Torte, 110
Brown Sugar Fudge Cake, 64
**Butterscotch**
  Butterscotch-Apple Crisp, 114
  Butterscotch Banana Bread, 74
  Butterscotch Brownies, 36
  Butterscotch-Nut Crêpes, 107
  Butterscotch People, 45
  Butterscotch Skillet Sauce,122
  Butterscotch Thins, 45
  Creamy Butterscotch Frosting, 124
  Heavenly Butterscotch Torte, 111

**Cakes.** See also Breakfast breads; Cheesecakes; Cupcakes; Tortes
  Brown Sugar Fudge, 64
  Chocolate Layer, 64
  Chocolate-Vanilla Swirl, 67
  Fudge Ribbon, 73
  Quick Party Log, 113
  Rich Devil's Food, 75
  Sachertorte, 66
  Sherry Fruitcake, 74
  Toll House Crumb, 17
  Toll House Bundt®, 19
**Candies and confections.** See also Fudge
  Blueberry Clusters, 53
  Bourbon Balls, 29
  Chocolate-Almond Bark, 30
  Chocolate Caramel Crowns, 30

Chocolate Clusters, 61
Chocolate-Covered Pretzels, 31
Chocolate-Dipped Fruit, 33
Chocolate-Mint Fancies, 25
Chocolate-Peanut Butter Cups, 26
Coconut Creams, 52
Creamy Chocolate Fudge, 33
Dipped Fruit Balls, 55
Easy Chocolate Fudge, 27
Fudge Drops, 26
Hopscotchers, 31
Marshmallow Cream Fudge, 29
Milk Chocolate Pralines, 54
Mix 'Ems, 51
Mocha-Rum Truffles, 22
Peanut Fudge Log, 60
Peppermint Creams, 52
Snow Caps, 23
Triple Treats, 27
Two-Tone Fudge, 22
Charlotte, Mocha, Frozen, 100
**Cheesecakes**
  Chocolate, 70
  Chocolate Swirl, 71
  Little Bits, 70
Cheese Crunchers, 37
Cherry Torte, Black Forest, 69
Chocolate, cooking with, 6
Chocolate-Almond Bark, 30
Chocolate-Almond Pie, 90
Chocolate Bavarian, 103
Chocolate Butter Frosting, 123
Chocolate Cappuccino Mousse Pie, 97
Chocolate Caramel Crowns, 30
Chocolate Cheesecake, 70
Chocolate Clusters, 61
Chocolate-Coconut Doughnuts, 77
Chocolate-Coconut Mousse Pie, 88
Chocolate Conversion Chart, 7
Chocolate-Covered Pretzels, 31
Chocolate Cream Pie, 83
Chocolate Crispies, 50
Chocolate Curls, 113
**Chocolate desserts.** See specific kind
Chocolate Dessert Waffles, 100
Chocolate-Dipped Fruit, 33
Chocolate-Dipped Shortbread Cookies, 44
Chocolate frostings and glazes, 119-26
Chocolate Layer Cake, 64
Chocolate Linzer Torte, 116
Chocolate-Meringue Nut Torte, 115
Chocolate-Mint Fancies, 25
Chocolate-Mint Soufflé, 94
Chocolate Mousse, 98
Chocolate-Nut Crêpes, 107
Chocolate-Orange Puffs, 96
Chocolate–Peanut Butter Brownies, 61
Chocolate–Peanut Butter Cups, 26
Chocolate Sandwich Cookies, 47

Chocolate sauces, 121, 122
Chocolate Shortbread, 42
Chocolate Skillet Sauce, 122
Chocolate Snappers, 46
Chocolate Soufflé, 106
Chocolate Surprise Coffeecake, 78
Chocolate Swirl Cheesecake, 71
Chocolate-Vanilla Swirl Cake, 67
Chocolate Velvet Pie, 90
**Coconut**
  Chocolate-Coconut Doughnuts, 77
  Chocolate-Coconut Mousse Pie, 88
  Creams, 52
**Coffeecakes.** See Breakfast breads
Cooked Chocolate Frosting, 123
**Cookies.** See also Brownies
  Butterscotch People, 45
  Butterscotch Thins, 45
  Cheese Crunchers, 37
  Chocolate Crispies, 50
  Chocolate-Dipped Shortbread, 44
  Chocolate Sandwich, 47
  Chocolate Shortbread, 42
  Chocolate Snappers, 46
  Magic Bars, 46
  Oatmeal Scotchies, 48
  Oatmeal Marble Squares, 48
  packing for mailing, 44
  Peanut Butter Burst, 54
  Peanut Butter Granola Cookies, 57
  Peanut Butter Jelly Bars, 57
  Toll House and variations, 10
  Toll House Treatwiches, 14
Cream Cheese Pie, Heavenly, 82
Cream Cheese Ripple Squares, 39
**Cream Puffs**
  Chocolate-Orange Puffs, 96
  Little Bits Cream Puffs, 58
Creamy Butterscotch Frosting, 124
Creamy Chocolate Fudge, 33
Creamy Mocha Frosting, 126
**Crêpes**
  Butterscotch-Nut, 107
  Chocolate-Nut, 107
  Party Chocolate, 108
Crumb Cake, Toll House, 17
**Cupcakes**
  Toll House, 16

Dipped Fruit Balls, 55
Double Chocolate Brownies, 13
Double Peanut Butter Brownies, 50
Doughnuts, Chocolate-Coconut, 77

Easy Chocolate Fondue, 116
Easy Chocolate Fudge, 27

Fondue Chocolate, Easy, 116
Frosted Fudge Brownies, 40
**Frostings**
  Chocolate Butter, 123

Cooked Chocolate, 123
Creamy Butterscotch, 124
Creamy Mocha, 126
Rich and Creamy Chocolate, 124
Rich Chocolate Cream, 126
Sour Cream Velvet, 124
tips about, 67
Frozen Mocha Charlotte, 100
**Fruit.** *See also specific kind*
Balls, Dipped, 55
Chocolate-Dipped, 33
**Fruitcakes**
Sherry, 74
**Fudge**
Chocolate, Easy, 27
Creamy Chocolate, 33
Drops, 26
Log, Peanut, 60
Marshmallow Cream, 29
Two-Tone, 22
Fudge Drops, 26
Fudge Ribbon Cake, 73

**Garnishes**
Chocolate Curls, 113
Meringue Mushrooms, 106
Golden Peanut Butter Brownies, 16
Granola Coffee Ring, 79
Grasshopper Pie, 84
Grasshopper Tarts, 83

Heavenly Butterscotch Torte, 111
Heavenly Cream Cheese Pie, 82
Hopscotchers, 31
Hot Chocolate, Rich, 110
Hot Chocolate Sauce, 121
Hot Creamy Fudge Sauce, 121
Hot Mocha Ice Cream Sauce, 122

**Ice Cream**
Blender Chocolate, 103

Layer Cake, Chocolate, 64
Little Bits Cheesecake, 70
Little Bits Cream Puffs, 58

Magic Bars, 46
Marshmallow Cream Fudge, 29
Meringue Mushrooms, 106
Milk Chocolate Pecan Bars, 41
Milk Chocolate Pralines, 54
Milk Chocolate Skillet Sauce, 122
Mint
Chocolate-Mint Fancies, 25
Chocolate-Mint Soufflé, 94
Peppermint Creams, 52
Mix 'Ems, 51
**Mocha desserts.** *See specific kind*
Mocha Ice Cream Sauce, Hot, 122
Mocha-Rum Truffles, 22
Mocha Soufflé, 94
**Mousses**
Blender, 98
Chocolate, 98
Mocha, 98

Oatmeal Marble Squares, 48
Oatmeal Scotchies, 48
Orange-Butterscotch Sauce, 121
Orange Puffs, Chocolate-, 96
Original Toll House Cookies, and variations, 10

Packing cookies for mailing, 44
Party Chocolate Crêpes, 108
Party Log, Quick, 113
Peanut Butter
Chocolate–Peanut Butter Brownies, 61
Chocolate–Peanut Butter Cups, 26
Double Peanut Butter Brownies, 50
Golden Peanut Butter Brownies, 16
Peanut Butter Burst Cookies, 54
Peanut Butter Granola Cookies, 57
Peanut Butter Hopscotchers, 31
Peanut Butter Jelly Bars, 57
Peanut Fudge Log, 60
Peanut Butter Granola Cookies, 57
Pears, Ruby, with Chocolate Cream, 101
Peppermint Creams, 52
**Pies**
Black Bottom, 89
Chocolate-Almond, 90
Chocolate Cappuccino Mousse, 97
Chocolate-Coconut Mousse, 88
Chocolate Cream, 83
Chocolate Velvet Pie, 90
Grasshopper, 84
Grasshopper Tarts, 83
Heavenly Cream Cheese, 82
Pumpkin Chiffon, 86
Toll House Walnut, 14
Pralines, Milk Chocolate, 54
Pressed Chocolate Shortbread, 42
Pretzels, Chocolate-Covered, 31
Pumpkin Chiffon Pie, 86

Quick Party Log, 113

Refrigerator Toll House Cookies, 12
Rich and Creamy Chocolate Frosting, 124
Rich Chocolate Cream Frosting, 126
Rich Devil's Food Cake, 75
Rich Hot Chocolate, 110
Ruby Pears with Chocolate Cream, 101

Sachertorte, 66
**Sauces**
Butterscotch Skillet, 122
Chocolate Skillet, 122
Hot Chocolate, 121
Hot Creamy Fudge, 121
Hot Mocha Ice Cream, 122

Milk Chocolate Skillet, 122
Orange-Butterscotch, 121
Sherry Fruitcake, 74
Snow Caps, 23
**Soufflés**
Chocolate, 106
Chocolate-Mint, 94
Mocha, 94
Sour Cream Velvet Frosting, 124

Toll House Bundt® Cake, 19
Toll House Cookies, 10
Toll House Crumb Cake, 17
Toll House Cupcakes, 16
Toll House Golden Brownies, 12
Toll House Treatwiches, 14
Toll House Walnut Pie, 14
**Tortes**
Black Forest Cherry, 69
Brownie, 110
Chocolate Linzer, 116
Chocolate-Meringue Nut, 115
Heavenly Butterscotch, 111
Sachertorte, 66
Triple-Layer Brownies, 36
Triple Treats, 27
Two-Tone Fudge, 22

Waffles, Dessert, Chocolate, 100
Walnut Pie, Toll House, 14
Whole Wheat Toll House Cookies, 10